Man Through the Ages

**Alexei Losev
Aza Takho-Godi**

# Aristotle

D1073516

**Progress Publishers**

Moscow

Translated from the Russian by *Angelia Graf*
Designed by *Vadim Novikov*

**А.Ф. Лосев, А.А. Тахо-Годи**
Аристотель
*На английском языке*

*Printed in the Union of Soviet Socialist Republics*

Л $\dfrac{0301030000-148}{014(01)-90}$ 35—90

ISBN 5-01-001985-X

# CONTENTS

4

# The Problem of the Living Aristotle

As authors of this book we face the complicated task of introducing the reader to the life and philosophy of the great Aristotle. However, we cannot wait for a final settlement of all problems. Scholarship never stands still. There may be a great many answers to the questions we have raised. But this, too, should not hinder our bringing forward the problems which we the authors consider timely and even essential given the contemporary state of scholarship. On the contrary, all these difficulties should only inspire us to overcome them. There will in any case never be a final resolution of all the difficulties connected with the study of Aristotle insofar as Aristotle himself is an endless topic for scholarly study.

The fact is that despite Aristotle's world-wide significance, the vital tendency of his philosophy and of his social and political activity was all too often underestimated in the past, and his philosophy was examined on an extremely abstract level without taking into account the living and palpitating sides of his thought. Even now many people find Aristotle's way of thinking and writing overly rational and completely forget the vital richness of his thought and activities. For our part we feel that the time has come to see the living Aristotle, and we shall try to depict the great philosopher in all the dynamism of his individual life path.

The opposition of life and of meaning, and in particular of life and the meaning of life, is very characteristic of everyday thinking, when people reason that life exists *per se* and its meaning also exists *per se*, can be compared with it and explain it. Such a position is diametrically opposed to both all ancient philosophy and, in particular, Aristotle. In Aristotle's view there is no life that is not permeated with meaning to its utmost depth, and no meaning which could be imagined separate from life. Later we shall see with what very deep meaning Aristotle's life was filled and how many riddles are hidden in this life, which only to poorly informed people appears simple or matter-of-course.

We shall also try to outline the basic principle of Aristotle's philosophy. It can be called a *general aesthetic* principle.

When we examine a painting or listen to music we immediately, without any scientific analysis, apprehend all the colors and sounds which the artist or composer has used, feeling an amazing closeness between the work of art and our thoughts and feelings. For art does not consist merely in colors and tones or life perceived through the senses. Art is also in one way or another always ideological, in other words it is an index of some kind of inner life, be it personal or socio-political or spiritual, but unfailingly of the inner life of a person and the inner life of the object portrayed in the art.

Close acquaintance with Aristotle will show the reader that everything that exists, in this philosopher's opinion, is nothing but a work of art. All of nature is also a work of art for Aristotle, and man himself is a work of art, and all the world with its sky and firmament is a work of art, too. It is no accident that the Greeks called the world the cosmos, for *cosmos* in Greek means harmony, concord, order, orderliness, and even beauty. In this respect Aristotle is a true ancient Greek. And none of his purely academic and abstract reasonings ever prevented him from seeing and feeling beauty as a principle of life's organization as a whole, whatever this life was like, good or bad. And this principle permeates all of life, from its very first steps to its summits.

Of course there were many thinkers who saw life and existence as based on the primacy of the aesthetic principle. But Aristotle did so in his own, highly original and diverse ways. And there is no point in undertaking the exposition and exploration of Aristotle's philosophy without the intention of understanding this primary aesthetic principle and appreciating its originality.

En route toward an aesthetic interpretation of reality Aristotle encountered a distorted interpretation of Plato[1] which at the time was widespread among Greek philosophers and which Plato himself would sometimes promote by extremely emphasizing and exaggerating certain aspects of his philosophical system, specifically his doctrine of the world of Ideas and the material world as a faint reflection of the Ideal world. It is true that Plato foresaw the distorted understanding of his doctrine of the Ideas as sharply opposed to the material world, and constantly pointed out that the Ideas cannot be isolated from the things, to give meaning to which is their only reason for existence, that they are necessary precisely to give meaning to these things.

Aristotle for his part observed the distortion of Plato's teaching that occurred when the ideas of things, existing somewhere in the unattainable heavens, were put in the foreground while the things themselves ended up being thrown into the world without any of their conceptual content. And Aristotle rose up with all the might of his philosophical talent against this severance of the idea from the thing. Of course the idea of the thing differs from the thing itself, Aristotle believed; and to a certain extent it can perfectly well exist in such an independent form as long as one observes scientific precision and theoretically fixes the gradual process of different degrees of interpenetration of the thing and its idea. However, according to Aristotle, in actuality it is quite impossible to sunder the one from the other and to set up a sharp opposition between things and ideas. Thus Aristotle himself did not deny the role of ideas in comprehending the material world but, taking a critical stance toward extreme idealism, he tried to use his own doctrine of the ideas for purely life-related purposes and for understanding all of reality as a work of art penetrated with the most profound ideological meaning. Let us note that V.I. Lenin regarded Aristotle's principled criticism of abstract Platonism in a very positive way: "Aristotle's criticism of Plato's 'ideas' is a criticism of *idealism as idealism in general*."[2]

In the *Philosophical Notebooks* Lenin wrote: "Hegel perceives the idealism of Aristotle in his idea of god. Of course, it is idealism, but more objective and *further removed, more general* than the idealism of Plato, hence in the philosophy of nature more frequently = materialism."[3]

One must note a highly original feature of Aristotle's thinking—the combination of a vital, all-embracing outlook on life with a detailed, scrupulous investigation of life down to the smallest trifles. Aristotle has an uncommon love of breaking up any general concept of an object, working it out in detail and singling out the subtlest nuances in it, and therefore in general describing reality in all

9

its infinite variety and complexity. On account of this analytical approach to objects and to life itself many students of Aristotle have seen in him traits of that philosophy that is negatively termed "scholastic".

However, one cannot fail to be astonished at how in spite of all his "scholasticism" Aristotle never lost his vital feeling for life.

Not by accident did Lenin write that in Aristotle's works could be found "a mass of extremely interesting, lively, *naive* (fresh) matter".[4] In Lenin's opinion, later on "the logic of Aristotle ... [was] made into a dead scholasticism by rejecting all the searchings, waverings and modes of framing questions".[5] Truly, after carefully studying all these apparently "scholastic", intellectual schemes and minutest details it becomes clear that Aristotle's perception of life is profound, vivid and convincing. The analytical scholar's approach to the subject of his philosophical study is indissolubly united with his keen experience of life. Such a conjunction of two seemingly incompatible methods may seem strange and surprising. But if one doesn't yield to one-sided, exaggerated and uncritical prejudices, one can only clap one's hands in delight at how masterfully Aristotle manages to join a dry, abstract expository style with a genuine enthusiasm for experiencing life.

The one-sided understanding of Aristotle as a dry and abstract philosopher was also connected with the fact that people usually completely forgot, first, his poetic works and, second, his epistolary legacy.

It is true that Aristotle composed few poems, but the little that he wrote is extremely interesting and revealing. As for his correspondence, although only a small portion of it has reached us, it is also a vivid testimony to Aristotle's fresh and varied perception of life and to his constant interest in not only theoretical and intellectual pursuits. Aristotle's poems and letters bear to us his living voice.

Following a long-established tradition people did not speak clearly enough about Aristotle's political activity and tried even less to conjoin his political activity with his philosophy in any meaningful way. Contemporary scholarship has at its disposal a whole series of studies of Aristotle specifically as a political figure. However, these works still do not go beyond the limits of a narrowly specialized study of the philosopher. In a book for the probing reader all the smallest indications and testimonies in ancient sources concerning his political activity must unfailingly be used to show what a tumultuous epoch Aristotle lived in, what were the unresolvable contradictions of the times, and what role history assigned Aristotle in this era. Without taking into account all of Aristotle's complex and dramatically full life, it is unthinkable to explain his philosophy and attempt any further exposition at all.

In studying Aristotle, one can in no way contrast such significant areas as his theory and his practice. In his theoretical views, especially in the realm of ethics, Aristotle is a proponent of an active life. Without conscious practical activity, according to Aristotle, man can never attain full satisfaction or happiness. However, this same Aristotle has very interesting thoughts on man's withdrawal into the depths of his own spirit and preaches that wisdom is a kind of aloofness from all the trifles of daily life.

While teaching that wisdom is self-introspection and independence from practical interest, Aristotle, as we have just said, was a very active person, taking bold steps which even professional politicians couldn't resolve upon. The amazing way in which Aristotle combined a philosophical aloofness of thought and a practical interest in life has also not always been attended to, and this question needs to be illuminated on the basis of ancient sources.

But we must formulate one more thesis without which Aristotle's fusion of theory and practice would remain essentially incomprehensible. Aristotle's uncommonly energetic nature came up against uncommonly difficult social and political conditions. Aristotle loved life very much and one can say was in love with life. But life could only place before Aristotle insoluble contradictions which in those times were beyond anyone's capacity to solve. And the life of Aristotle, this titan of human wisdom, was fated to have a tragic outcome.

Diogenes Laertius, the Greek writer and historian of ancient philosophy (third century AD), lists 445, 270 lines written by Aristotle (V, 21-28)[6]. Some of his works consisted of a large number of books (for example, his descriptions of the social structure of various city-states).

Hesychius of Alexandria (sixth century AD) adds to Diogenes Laertius' list 47 more titles of authentic works by Aristotle and 10 attributed to him. But he is of the opinion that Aristotle wrote 400 books. Another admirer and biographer of Aristotle, the philosopher Ptolemy, known from the references to him by Arab historians, says that Aristotle wrote thousands of works.

Apart from the works that have reached us in their entirety (leaving aside for the moment the question of the degree to which they reproduce the original text), fragments of above fifty more works have been preserved. These fragments contain from a few lines or simply some one expression to a few pages. The largest fragments remaining are from the dialogues "On Philosophy", "On the Good", "On the Soul", "On Poets"; from the works entitled "The Homeric Problems", "On the Ideas", "On the Pythagoreans", "Physical Problems"; from various zoological works (mainly thanks to the information provided by the third-century AD writer Athenaeus, who in his work "Dinnertable Philosophers" widely draws on materials from Aristotle, enumerating an unbelievable quantity of birds and fish which were used in ancient cooking); quite a few fragments remain from "The Athenian Constitution" and "The Spartan Constitution" (the concept included not only the constitution of the state, but also its way of life, history and economy). Few of Aristotle's letters and poems have survived.

Since to Aristotle are attributed works on all imaginable topics (except perhaps military arts), one gets the impression that a whole academy is hidden under this one name, especially if one considers that Aristotle writes in as much minute detail on the most specific problems of poetic devices, medical science or animal behavior as if he had studied nothing else his whole life.

As far as subject matter is concerned, Aristotle authored works on logic, metaphysics[7], natural philosophy[8], the natural sciences, ethics and artistic creation. We will not touch here on the question of the genuine and spurious parts of all these works and still less the question of the undoubtedly spurious works of Aristotle.

[1] *Plato*: the great ancient Greek philosopher of the fifth and fourth centuries BC. Plato's philosophy and life are outlined in Alexei Losev and Aza Takho-Godi, *Plato*, Progress Publishers, Moscow, 1990.

[2] V.I. Lenin, *Collected Works*, Progress Publishers, Moscow, 1976, 38: 281.

[3] Ibid., p. 280.

[4] Ibid., p. 365.

[5] Ibid., pp. 366-67.

[6] "In all 445,270 lines. Such is the number of the works written by him." Diogenes Laertius, *Lives of Eminent Philosophers*, William Heinemann Ltd., London, 1938, I: 475.

The works of ancient authors consisted of so-called books, i.e., strictly speaking, parts, which in turn were divided into smaller parts—chapters and paragraphs. Here and subsequently the numbers cited in parentheses give the source from which the information or quote is taken: a Roman numeral indicates the number of the book, an Arabic numeral, the chapter or paragraph. When examples are cited from works of Aristotle (or other authors) which have reached us in fragments, the Arabic numeral in parentheses indicates the number of the fragment (cf. p. 21).

Plato's works are cited in the traditional style: the Roman numeral indicates the book, the Arabic numeral, the page, and the Latin letter, the page division (cf. p. 41).

[7] *Metaphysics*: teachings on Being and the higher forces above nature which rule it.

[8] *Natural philosophy*: philosophy of nature.

# MAIN WORKS OF ARISTOTLE

**ON BEING**
*Metaphysics* (on the "first philosophy"), 13 books
*Physics*, 8 books
*On the Heavens*
*On Beginning and Perishing*, 2 books

**LOGIC** (the "Organon")
*Categories*
*On Interpretation*
*Prior Analytics*
*Posterior Analytics*
*Topics* (the last section of this treatise is sometimes published separately under the title *On Sophistical Refutations*)

**PSYCHOLOGY**
*On the Soul*

**ETHICS**
*Nicomachean Ethics*, 10 books
*Eudemian Ethics*
*Magna Moralia*

**ART**
*Poetics*
*Rhetoric*, 3 books

**POLITICS**
*Politics*, 8 books

**HISTORY**
*The Athenian Constitution* (the state structure of Athens)

**NATURAL SCIENCES**
*Meteorologics* (on atmospheric phenomena)
*On the Parts of Animals*, 4 books
*On the Movement of Animals*
*On the Generation of Animals*
*Historia Animalium*

# I

# Aristotle Before His Appearance in Plato's Academy (384/3 – 367/6 BC)

## Macedonia

Aristotle's life and personality are linked with Macedonia, near which he was born. During the whole of the fourth century BC it played an increasingly decisive role in the life of the Greek people. It was a country to the north of the area which is usually called Northern Greece, i.e., to the north of Epirus and Thessaly. The Macedonians were so closely connected with Thrace and Illyria even farther north that it is still a big question for specialists what purely Greek elements and what Thracian and Illyrian elements lie at the origin of the Macedonian nation.

Some think that Macedonia is a sort of offshoot of ancient Greece close to Thessaly. Others try to maximally separate the Macedonians from the Greeks. Still others feel that both Greek and Thracio-Illyrian elements were equally represented in the so-called substratum of the Macedonian people. It is not part of our task to engage in the solution of this problem with all its ethnic and linguistic difficulties. Nevertheless, two circumstances are immediately obvious, irrespective of our scholarly interests in the historical origins of Macedonia.

The first circumstance is that however distant the Macedonians were from the Greeks in cultural terms, nonetheless the successes of Greek culture and the enormous achievements of Greek civilization always impressed the Macedonians, so that the Macedonian rulers strove to assimilate the achievements of Greek culture, preferred the Greeks to all other peoples and historically always tried to keep in step with them.

The second circumstance consists in what could be called opposition to Greece. The Macedonians were not Barbarians in the eyes of Greece or their own eyes. But it was their constant dream to become greater than Greece politically and militarily. It was not a Barbaric urge to destroy Greek civilization. On the contrary, the Macedonians always considered themselves the pupils of the Greeks. And yet the Macedonians' conquest of Greece occurred even before they headed for Asia. True, their respect for the Greeks persisted even here, in that they were much gentler with respect to the Greeks and gave them much greater political freedom. Nevertheless, the Macedonian rulers had from time immemorial fixed their gaze on Greece and tried to snatch one or another part of it. Particularly successful in this respect were two famous Macedonian kings: Philip II (c. 382-336 BC) and his son Alexander (356-323 BC), who while still young, conquered almost the entire civilized world of the time up to India.

### Aristotle's Origins

Aristotle, the son of Nicomachus and Phaestis, was born in 384/3 BC, and more precisely, between July and October 384. This was the first year of the 99th Olympiad. It must be noted, however, that the Greeks began their chronology with the supposed first year of the first Olympiad, i.e., 776 BC. The word *Olympiad* itself arose to designate the four-year interval between Olympic Games, which got their name from Olympus in the Western Peloponnesus where the national Greek games were held. Therefore when in Greek sources we find references to this or that Olympiad, the designation is not very exact for us since it embraces a whole four years. But we have exact knowledge of Aristotle's birth precisely in the first year of the 99th Olympiad.

The name of the town in which Aristotle was born can also be rendered in various ways: we will use the form Stagira. In both ancient and world literature Aristotle is also called the Stagirite, i.e., born in Stagira.

From the point of view of Greeks of the time not only Stagira but all of Macedonia was a rather remote province, which in the northeast even bordered on Thrace. According to some sources, Stagira was actually located in Thrace. But we proceed from the assumption that Stagira was located in southern Macedonia, on a peninsula called Chalcidice near the much better known and subsequently quite significant city of Thessalonica. Stagira was founded by immigrants from the island of Andros (this was the homeland of Aristotle's father; people also said that Aristotle's paternal ancestors came from Messana — present-day Messina — in Sicily, which was a colony of Euboean Chalcis) and from Euboean Chalcis, the home of Aristotle's maternal ancestors (the island of Andros was only a few miles away from the island of Euboea).

From all this it follows that despite the geographic proximity to Macedonia of his birthplace Stagira, Aristotle was purely Greek on both his father and mother's sides. His parents, for reasons unknown to us, settled in Macedonia, on the Chalcidice Peninsula. But this circumstance noticeably complicates our understanding of Aristotle's very strong pro-Macedonian sympathies. As we shall see, these sympathies played a huge part in his life. The Macedonian rulers, as admirers of Greek culture, were always at odds with themselves: they learned from the Greeks in order to be at the peak of the culture of their day, but at the same time they always dreamed of subjugating Greece to their power. Hence, too, came the profound contradiction which tormented Aristotle and which, as we shall see, led him to a tragic end. Let us note, however, that this sort of contradictory situation is not at all some exceptional rarity in history.

A little later great Rome would also consider itself a disciple of Greek culture. But this same Rome would subjugate Greece like any other country of the then civilized world.

Now let us turn to one more very important circumstance connected with the philosopher's origin.

His highly provincial origin was compensated for by the fact that he was the son of the famous doctor Nicomachus. And here it is appropriate to mention that Aristotle's father did not simply belong to a family of hereditary doctors. The medical profession was highly respected and honored among the ancient Greeks. All doctors, the Greeks believed, were descended from the divine physician Asclepius, the son of none other than Apollo himself and a mortal woman, or maybe even the nymph Coronis. Asclepius was so skilled in the art of medicine that Zeus killed him with a lightning-bolt out of fear that he would make all humans immortal.

Here was a whole, rather tangled myth. Coronis, beloved by Apollo, married a certain Ischys, son of the Thessalonian king Elatus. Out of jealousy Apollo killed Coronis, but tore from her womb the infant about to be born and named him Asclepius. Asclepius was educated by the wise centaur Chiron (Pindar, *The Pythian Odes* III, 45-54).[1] Asclepius' medical art led him to the audacious thought of resurrecting the dead. Myths tell of his resurrection of many heroes: Hippolytus, Capaneus, Glaucus, the son of Minos, and others. The enraged Zeus struck him with a lightning-bolt (Apollodorus III, 10, 3-4). In response Apollo killed the Cyclopes, Zeus' blacksmiths, and was sent by Zeus to expiate his guilt in the service of mankind. Two sons are ascribed to Asclepius, Machaon and Podaleirius, who are mentioned as fine physicians as far back as Homer (*Iliad* IV, 194; XI, 518).[2] Asclepius' wife was named Epione, which means Soother of Pain, and his daughters were called Hygieia (Health) and Panacea (Universal Healer).

The cult of Asclepius was particularly famous in the city of Epidaurus, where people thronged from all corners of Greece to have their illnesses cured. In his comedy *The Plutus* (654-741), despite the parodic situation, Aristophanes brings in information on how at night, while they were asleep, pilgrims were cured in the temple of Asclepius.[3] Asclepius' indispensable attribute was a snake, which received sacrifices in the temple.

The figure of Asclepius combines ancient, i.e., chthonic[4] forces of the healing earth (hence the snake living in the depths of the earth; moreover not only is the snake an attribute of Asclepius, but he himself is thought of as a snake) and the notion that divine functions were transmitted to the sons of gods, heroes who in their audacity violated the balance established in the world by the gods inhabiting Olympus.

Those who are not particularly versed in ancient mythology might wonder how it is that Asclepius, a god, could be killed. His killing must be understood in the same sense in which Uranus was "killed" by Cronus, and Cronus and all the Titans were "killed" by Zeus. This was not killing in the proper sense of the word, but simply the removal from divine power or overthrow into the underworld of Tartarus. The huge importance of these prisoners of Tartarus not only did not decrease but on the contrary increased and simply took on another sense, that of a mighty force hidden deep in the bowels of the earth. In turn these deep-seated forces of the earth tried to exert an influence on humans, in opposition to the Olympian gods. That is why one of the Titans, Prometheus, was considered a protector of humans and the originator of human civilization. Similarly, Asclepius' killing through the malevolence of Zeus brought him closer to humans and led to a conception of him as a defender and healer of the unfortunate, the god and patron of medical arts.

Thus, the worship of Asclepius was rooted in ancient myth. And to be descended from Asclepius meant occupying a prominent position in society. The famous doctors on the island of Kos considered themselves descendants of the god and were called Asclepids.

Descent from Asclepius was part of Aristotle's family tradition. It is not at all important in this case that notions of this kind were fantastic in nature. They were no fable for either the ancient Greeks or, specifically, Aristotle. Aristotle seriously believed himself to be a distant descendant of Asclepius. And from a historical perspective this is very important.

The old tradition represented Aristotle too abstractly and intellectually. He was usually portrayed as a rationalist, a professor who lived only for his academic research. In reality he was a very lively and artistically inclined thinker who in a remarkable way combined his philosophical and scientific work with the naive religious and mythological inclinations of his people. Belief in a divine ancestor did not at all impede his activity as a sober and energetic politician. The conjunction of mythological conceptions and practical life experience was generally characteristic of the classical ancient Greeks and closely linked Aristotle with his contemporaries and compatriots.

Incidentally, not the least important fact by far in this whole mythical genealogy of Aristotle is Asclepius' previously mentioned training in the medical arts under the centaur Chiron, a son of Cronus, who was the mentor and most wise tutor of many Greek heroes, first and foremost Achilles. And Cronus was one of the Titans, the sons of Uranus (the Sky) and Gaea (the Earth), in other words belonged to the older generation of gods.

All these circumstances indicate how much the ancient Greeks valued the medical arts and with what ancient gods they connected them. Of course the Greek physicians were not a special class, on the order of an aristocracy. But from our point of view they were a special kind of intelligentsia. Aristotle's father Nicomachus, son of Nicomachus, was a descendant of the Nicomachus considered to be the son of Machaon, and, as we know, Machaon was the son of the god Asclepius. Aristotle's Arab biographers speak of a few Nicomachuses between Machaon and Aristotle's father Nicomachus. We can read in Pausanias, a writer of late antiquity, that the first Nicomachus was the son of the famous doctor Machaon (IV, 3, 1-2, 9-10).[5] It is characteristic that both Machaon and his son Nicomachus were worshipped in Messana, where a special cult of them was established.

In ancient Greece being a doctor meant occupying a high social position. Since there were no pharmacies, physicians also compounded and prepared medicines, and often invented them as well. There is no doubt that in the most ancient period Greek medicine originally had a religious character and was often based on various kinds of superstitions. But the renowned Greek doctor Hippocrates from the island of Kos had already made himself famous in the fifth century BC, one hundred years before Aristotle's birth. Hippocrates had made a mass of empirical observations and left behind all kinds of important instructions on real ways of curing illnesses. It is therefore not surprising that Aristotle's father, an inhabitant of the provincial town of Stagira, was so well known throughout Macedonia that he was invited to serve as a court physician to King Amyntas II, father of the famous Philip II and grandfather of the even more famous Alexander the Great.

And yet it must be said that Aristotle had a very democratic attitude to his "divine" origin. A whole discourse has come down to us in which he argues that noble origin does not at all consist in wealth or simply in one's ancestors' prowess, but exclusively in valor which has been handed down from ancient times and utterly defines the whole clan, insofar as each member of the tribe multiplies this valor with his own personal talents (fragment 94).

Nicomachus lived at the Macedonian court with his wife Phaestis and three children: his sons Aristotle and Arimnestus and his daughter Arimnesta. (The ancient capital of Macedonia was the city of Aegae. Later on Philip moved the capital to Pella.) After Nicomachus' death between 376/5 and 367 BC, his whole family returned to Stagira from Pella. Nicomachus was also connected by ties of friendship with King Amyntas. Scholars of the late ancient world ascribed to Aristotle's father works on medicine and natural philosophy, i.e., considered him to have been not only a practising physician but also a theoretician of medicine.

### Aristotle's Relatives

After his parents' death the future great philosopher was brought up by a certain Proxenus. Very little is known of this man. We know that he was the second husband of Aristotle's older sister Arimnesta, who bore him a son called Nicanor. According to some sources, Proxenus was an acquaintance or even a friend of Plato, and possibly even Hermeias of Atarneus, of whom we shall speak later. Proxenus came from the city of Atarneus, which was located in the coastal area of Mysia in Asia Minor, and later moved to Stagira. According to the philosopher Sextus Empiricus (who was also a doctor, by the way), Proxenus was even born in Stagira and was a blood relative of Aristotle. There are some noteworthy accounts, not very reliable, however, that Proxenus took Aristotle to Athens and supposedly even turned him over to be educated and instructed by Plato.

### Appearance and Character

Since youth Aristotle is said to have been unprepossessing in appearance. He was scrawny and had skinny legs, tiny eyes and a lisp. In compensation he liked to dress up, wore several expensive rings at a time and styled his hair in an unusual way.

Concerning his social habits it must be said that they are hardly of much significance. Certainly these habits of a renowned philosopher may make a strange impression. But the accounts of Aristotle's foppishness relate to his youth, and that is excusable. We won't be too captious.

For example, one may risk assuming that Aristotle was a rather vain and ambitious man, especially in his later years. He is known to have been displeased with the decisions taken against him in Delphi. He considered them unworthy of his fame. He even complained about them to Antipater, Alexander the Great's viceroy in Greece. The source which provides this information, and which does not charge Aristotle with vanity, is most instructive. In the *Varia Historia* of the second-century AD writer Aelian (XIV, 1), we read that Aristotle, justly considered a wise man, after being deprived of the honors appointed him in Delphi wrote to Antipater that as far as the honors that had been allotted him in Delphi and now rescinded were concerned, he had decided not to think about them too much but not to stop thinking about them entirely either. Aelian goes on to say that these words do not attest to Aristotle's vainglory and that he would not accuse him of anything of the sort, since Aristotle was fully justified in thinking that it is quite a different matter not to have something at all, and to have it and then lose it; for it isn't terrible not to get something in the first place, but it is painful to be deprived of what one has already got.

All these brief bits of information about Aristotle's personality are only preliminary in character. In the course of our exposition we will have many occasions yet to encounter other much more important aspects of the great philosopher's personality.

### Major and Minor Points in the Biography
### of the Young Aristotle

In 367/6 BC Aristotle decided to go to Athens. Unreliable versions which were given the lie by their own narrators, proclaimed that Aristotle ran through his inheritance in Athens, engaged in quack healing and doctoring, and was even a soldier. Aelian comes right out and says that in his youth Aristotle squandered his father's legacy and was forced to become a soldier, but had to ingloriously abandon this life and become a dealer in medicinal drugs. Having made his way unnoticed to the *Peripat*[6], by listening to the philosophical conversations there he, thanks to his exceptional gifts, acquired the rudiments of the knowledge which he later mastered completely (V, 9).[7]

Although he was brought up in a doctor's family and therefore studied medicine himself, Aristotle did not become a professional physician. But throughout his life medicine remained such a homely and familiar field to him that in his most difficult philosophical treatises he often explains some profound theory with examples drawn from medical practice. Moreover he unquestionably had a scientific attitude to medicine and was highly critical of doctors' advice. Again we find Aelian telling us that the Pythagoreans were reported to have assiduously practised the art of doctoring, while Plato, Aristotle son of Nicomachus, and many others also paid lavish tribute to it (IX, 22). Elsewhere he describes how Aristotle was sick one day. When the doctor gave him some prescriptions he told him not to treat him like a shepherd or a ploughman, but first to explain why he was giving them and then he would be ready to listen. Thus the philosopher demonstrated his unwillingness to follow prescriptions without knowing the reasons behind them (IX, 23).

Thus, from a young age Aristotle had a good knowledge of medicine and a favorable but at the same time quite critical attitude toward its prescriptions.

Generally speaking there is a quantity of all sorts of sources for Aristotle's biography which often contradict each other and require a critical approach. For instance, one source proclaims that Aristotle first came to Athens as an eight-year-old boy, supposedly brought there by Proxenus, the husband of Aristotle's sister Arimnesta. This testimony undoubtedly originated in a desire to say something about Aristotle's studies before Plato's Academy, to acknowledge him to have been already schooled to some extent before his tutelage under Plato. But this is probably only a conjecture, since the remaining sources speak of Aristotle's arrival in Athens at the age of seventeen or eighteen. One must bear in mind that Aristotle could very well have managed without any particular preparation and have appeared in the Academy without any preliminary schooling. It is possible that he studied as stipulated by tradition and regulations, but specifically how and where is not known for sure. In the final analysis this is not all that important. The fact of Aristotle's entrance into the Academy is much more interesting from our point of view. And this fact nobody denies.

It was further said that even before joining the Academy Aristotle had studied rhetoric, that he was a pupil of the famous rhetorician Isocrates (436-338 BC) and that he ended up in the Academy only at the age of thirty after becoming disenchanted with rhetoric. It is not at all out of the question that Aristotle studied under Isocrates. But once again, even if he did, this fact is not as important as his enrollment in Plato's Academy and his extensive literary activity while still at the Academy.

Incidentally, the question of Aristotle's attendance at Isocrates' school is no simple one; here, too, it seems, one can draw some connections between Aristotle's rhetorical interests and his youthful studies.

First of all, Isocrates' school of rhetoric was famous at the time and better known and more popular than even Plato's school. Isocrates had founded it around 393 BC, i.e., at least five or six years before the Academy was started. Other sources have it that both schools arose at the same time. The outstanding rhetorician Isocrates began to attract students from all over Greece; and it would not be in the least surprising if Aristotle had turned first to him.

Furthermore, study of Aristotle's philosophy testifies to his great love for rhetoric, while his specialized treatise *Rhetoric* betokens his vast experience and erudition in this area and his love for rhetorical investigations. Even in his theoretical philosophy Aristotle assigned an important place to rhetoric; and he directly calls his basic method of logical investigations, which he advocates in his treatise *Topics*, a rhetorical one. It is also known that when he entered the Academy he was entrusted with giving a special course of lectures specifically on rhetoric. And if some biographical accounts attest to Aristotle's differences with Isocrates, the originality of Aristotle's thinking makes this deviation only natural. Aristotle's first compositions while at the Academy are also characterized by a penchant for rhetoric. Let us note that in his youth Isocrates had been in Larissa in northern Greece, where he was in contact with Gorgias (483-380 BC), who was famed not only as a sophist but also as a talented orator. Hence it is also possible that Aristotle studied rhetoric while he was still in the north, before his arrival in Athens.

Theoretically speaking, it is therefore quite likely that Aristotle attended Isocrates' school. But compared to his enrollment in Plato's Academy this fact is naturally of secondary importance to us. After all it is possible, on the other hand, that Aristotle's classical and Arab biographers didn't know how to fill in the three years between Aristotle's arrival in Athens and his meeting with Plato, which could not have occurred earlier than 365/4 BC. (As is known, Plato spent these three years in Sicily for philosophical and political purposes.) And in view of Aristotle's clear and continuing interest in rhetoric in his maturity as well as in his youth, preliminary study in Isocrates' famous and popular school was regarded as more than probable. For us now, the most important fact is the young Aristotle's enrollment in Plato's school.

There is no point in getting carried away over various problematic points in Aristotle's early biography, particularly when they are given contradictory interpretations in the sources. One thing is important to us: having come from the north of Greece under this or that circumstance, Aristotle entered Plato's school at a very early age; at first he adhered to the principles of Platonic philosophy, but later departed from strict Platonism.

That is an indisputable and important fact in Aristotle's biography.

### NOTES

[1] *The Odes of Pindar,* Harvard University Press, Cambridge, 1978, p. 189.
[2] *The Complete Works of Homer,* the Modern Library, New York, s. a., pp. 64, 200.

[3]*The Comedies of Aristophanes,* George Bell and Sons, London, 1907, VI: 73-83.

[4]From the Greek word *chthon*: earth.

[5]Pausanias, *Description of Greece*, Harvard University Press, Cambridge, 1977, II: 181-83, 187-89.

[6]*Peripat*: a place for strolling in the suburbs of Athens (cf. pp. 79-80).

[7]The second-century AD philosopher Aristocles traces this view of Aristotle's early youth back to Epicurus. Extracts from Aristocles' works are found in the late Greek writer Eusebius of Caeseria (265-340 AD). However, the accounts of Aristotle's turbulent youth can be disputed, as they were by Aristocles himself.

# II

## At Plato's Academy (367/6-348/7 BC)

### Enrollment in Plato's Academy

Let us consider it true that in the eighteenth year of his life Aristotle entered the Academy and became a faithful disciple of Plato. This circumstance alone, despite the lack of any evidence concerning Aristotle's spiritual development in his early years, testifies to his enormous inner needs in his youthful period, to his extensive learning and his philosophical interests, which led him to none less than the famous Plato. For by that time Plato was already known to the whole philosophical and even non-philosophical world from Asia Minor and Egypt to Sicily.

Thus, the son of a doctor made his appearance in the Academy at the age of eighteen to become a faithful disciple of Plato. However, Aristotle did not immediately meet Plato there since the head of the Academy was in Sicily at that time.

Plato's three trips to Sicily can be called ill-fated in the full sense of the word. The fact was that for many years Plato had dreamed of founding an ideal state, such as he had written of in his special treatise entitled *The Republic*. At the head of such a state, in Plato's view, were the philosophers, contemplating the eternal Ideas and wisely governing the society on this basis. The second class in Plato's ideal state consisted of the warriors, who had no private property, lived ascetically and defended the state from internal and external enemies. The third class was made up of the farmers and artisans, whose task was to feed the entire state but who in return enjoyed personal freedom. Plato's Sicilian friends, despite his own scepticism, several times tried to get him to come to Sicily, where, so it seemed to his disciples, it would be possible to establish an ideal state. Plato had undertaken his first trip to Sicily

27

back in the 390's; but all kinds of intrigues at the court of King Dionysius I (the Elder) of Syracuse, the ruler of Sicily at the time, led to Plato's being sold into slavery. (His freedom was, however, immediately bought back by his friends.) And now, in 366 BC, Plato again left for Sicily at the urgent invitation of his faithful disciple Dion, one of the political figures at the court of the new ruler of Sicily, Dionysius the Younger. Dionysius II turned out to be even more of a cruel and willful tyrant than his father. Under his rule Plato was not only unable to undertake anything in Sicily, but even in danger of death and barely escaped from Syracuse alive, for all the apparent favor acted out for him by Dionysius II. Nonetheless, Plato spent about three years in Sicily this time and returned to Athens only in 364 BC. His place as head of the Academy had been filled during this time by Eudoxus of Cnidos (408-355 BC), whom we shall speak of again later. It was during Eudoxus' administration that Aristotle entered the Academy. After Plato's return in 364 BC, Aristotle met him and they remained in association right up to Plato's death in 347 BC, i.e., for seventeen years.

## Aristotle's Differences with Plato at the Academy

Specialists on Aristotle have always been interested in the question of Aristotle and Plato's mutual closeness and mutual differences. We shall discuss the theoretical views of both philosophers below. Here we shall describe the external and to a significant extent purely social side of this question.

Some ancient sources speak directly not only of the divergences but even hostility between the two great philosophers.

Truly, Aristotle's great concern for his own appearance, which we mentioned earlier, disgusted Plato, who naturally considered this sort of behavior, even on the part of a young man, quite inappropriate in a genuine philosopher.

We find an interesting account of the matter once again in Aelian, who writes that the following cause was attributed to Plato's enmity toward Aristotle. Plato did not approve of Aristotle's characteristic bearing and dress. For Aristotle attached too much importance to his clothing and footwear, cut his hair short, unlike Plato, and liked to flaunt his numerous rings. There was something arrogant in his face, and his volubility, moreover, pointed to a vain disposition. Needless to say such qualities are not proper of a true philosopher. Therefore Plato avoided Aristotle's company, preferring Xenocrates, Speusippus and others, whom he singled out in all manner of ways, in particular by allowing them to take part in his philosophical conversations (III, 19).

Apparently in his youth Aristotle really did like to show off with his costumes, his speech, and all his outer conduct in general, which could not but cause irritation in older and steadier people. True, in his mature works Aristotle depicts the philosopher immersed in spiritual questing, far from all external trifles of daily life. But he probably entered Plato's Academy still with the habits of his early youth. As far as can be judged, he had a rather refractory temper. Plato, of course, understood this well, as ancient sources also confirm: "He [Xenocrates] was naturally slow and clumsy. Hence Plato, comparing him to Aristotle, said, 'The one needed a spur, the other a bridle.' And again, 'See what an ass I am training and what a horse he has to run against.'(IV.6)"[1] Consequently, Plato saw Aristotle as a spirited horse which constantly needed to be held in check.

But as if this weren't enough, Aristotle evidently also impertinently attacked Plato, an attitude which later led to his founding of his own school. On account of these arguments with him, the good-natured Plato called Aristotle a colt kicking its own mother. We have several informants on this point. Plato called Aristotle a colt, says Aelian, going on to ask why he chose this nickname, and answering that colts are known to lash out at their dams when they have nursed their fill: thus did Plato hint at Aristotle's ingratitude; for having received the most important foundations of knowledge from Plato, he cast off the bridle after mastering these treasures, opened his own school opposite Plato's, strolled around there with his students and friends and became an inveterate opponent of his teacher (IV, 9). Reports Diogenes Laertius: "He seceded from the

Academy while Plato was still alive. Hence the remark attributed to the latter: 'Aristotle spurns me, as colts kick out at the mother who bore them'" (V, 2).

Some of Aristotle's enemies had even worse to say. According to Diogenes Laertius, Eubulides of Miletus, a spokesman of the Megarian school, "kept up a controversy with Aristotle and said much to discredit him" (II, 109), while Eusebius (quoting Aristocles) would tell how Aristotle didn't even come to Plato on his deathbed and marred his books.

It is hard to say what is meant by this marring and whether it refers to the text of Plato's works or to Aristotle's commentaries. Aristocles, however, casts doubt on the truthfulness of reports of this nature.

In any event, Aristotle's hostility toward Plato, not without petty elements even, was felt within the walls of the Academy. There probably was something dubious about Aristotle's behavior after all. Spiteful tongues claimed that he had bathed in warm oil and then sold the oil (Diogenes Laertius citing Lyco, V, 16). People also said that Aristotle had ousted Plato from the place in the Academy where he taught, taking advantage of the illness of Speusippus, Plato's nephew, and the absence of Xenocrates, another of Plato's favorite students. Aelian (III, 19) tells us that one day, when Xenocrates had left Athens for a while to visit his native town, Aristotle accompanied by Mnaso of Phocaea and others went up to Plato and began to press him. Speusippus was sick that day and could not accompany his teacher, an eighty-year-old man with a memory already weakened by age. Aristotle maliciously attacked him and arrogantly began to ask him questions, wishing to expose him somehow, and behaved impertinently and most disrespectfully. From that time on Plato ceased to go outside the limits of his own garden and strolled around with his pupils only within the enclosure.

At the end of three months Xenocrates returned and found Aristotle walking where Plato had used to. Noticing that after their walk he headed with his companions not for Plato's house but for town, he asked one of Aristotle's interlocutors where Plato was, because he thought that Plato had not come out on account of illness. The man answered that Plato was in good health but since Aristotle had insulted him he had stopped walking there and carried on conversations with his students in his own garden. Hearing this, Xenocrates immediately went to Plato's home and found him surrounded by a great many listeners, all worthy and well-known people. At the end of his conversation, Plato welcomed Xenocrates with his usual cordiality and the latter responded no less warmly; at this meeting neither uttered a word about what had happened. Afterwards Xenocrates assembled Plato's students and started angrily scolding Speusippus for yielding the place where they usually strolled, then attacked Aristotle and acted so resolutely that he drove him away and returned to Plato the place where he was accustomed to teach.

## Marks of Respect for Plato

This sort of behavior at the Academy is evidently connected with Aristotle's refractory temperament, of which Plato himself spoke on several occasions. More important are the philosophical divergences between teacher and student. But regardless of his differences with Plato over many philosophical issues, Aristotle did not at all think of leaving the Academy and removed from it only after Plato's death. For Aristotle is known to have given lectures and conducted classes in the Academy, as he naturally could not have done without Plato's permission.

Even in those cases where Aristotle does not agree with Plato, he frequently says not "I" but "we", counting himself among the students of Plato's school (*Metaphysics* I, 8, 9; III, 2, 6).[2] This means that regardless of his differences with Plato, Aristotle nevertheless reckoned himself part of his school, considered himself a Platonist.

Furthermore, in his *Nicomachean Ethics* (I, 6), Aristotle writes: "We had perhaps better consider the universal good and discuss thoroughly what is meant by it, although such an inquiry is made an uphill one by the fact that the Forms have been introduced by friends of our own. Yet it would perhaps be thought to be better, indeed to be our duty, for the sake of maintaining the truth even to destroy what touches us closely, especially as we are

31

philosophers or lovers of wisdom; for, while both are dear, piety requires us to honor truth above our friends."[3] It seems to us that insofar as these words refer to Plato, one can draw only the most positive conclusion from them concerning the two philosophers' personal relations. After all, it is not all that rare for people to be very close and yet differ in their theoretical views. Incidentally, the phrase about Plato being a friend but truth being dearer became a saying which is still current today. The word "truth" is usually emphasized here, as it should be. When we use this phrase we don't think of Plato at all but of whoever it may be in general. But in Aristotle's mouth the whole expression relates not only to the truth but also to Plato himself, his very close and only teacher. To be sure, for Aristotle the word "truth" also incorporates something great and universally human. He begins his *Metaphysics* with the words: "All men by nature desire to know" (I, 1). But this knowledge of things is the knowledge of their causes, and the knowledge of eternal things is the knowledge of eternal causes (II, 1). As he says in his *Rhetoric* (I, 1), "...it may also be noted that men have a sufficient natural instinct for what is true, and usually do arrive at the truth... Things that are true and things that are just have a natural tendency to prevail over their opposites."[4] Furthermore, "The investigation of the truth is in one way hard, in another easy. An indication of this is found in the fact that no one is able to attain the truth adequately, while, on the other hand, we do not collectively fail, but every one says something true about the nature of things, and while individually we contribute little or nothing to the truth, by the union of all a considerable amount is amassed" (*Metaphysics* II, 1). In *On the Soul* (I, 1), he writes: "Holding as we do that, while knowledge of any kind is a thing to be honored and prized, one kind of it may, either by reason of its greater exactness or of a higher dignity and greater wonderfulness in its objects, be more honorable and precious than another, on both accounts we should naturally be led to place in the front rank the study of the soul." And again in his *Rhetoric* (I, 11): "Learning things and wondering at things are also pleasant as a rule; wondering implies the desire of learning, so that the object of

32

wonder is an object of desire; while in learning one is brought into one's natural condition."

In addition to what has been said above, let us cite an interesting reference in Ammonius (fifth century AD), a late commentator on Plato and Aristotle, according to whom Plato called Aristotle's dwelling the house of the reader (probably an indication of Aristotle's great interest in reading and reciting, perhaps even in Plato's works, or in giving lectures). A student of this same Ammonius, Philoponus, informs us in turn that Plato called Aristotle the mind of discussion, the Greek word which we render as "discussion" having a much broader meaning of human intercourse.

It is also notable that while at the Academy Aristotle became close to the Xenocrates mentioned earlier. Xenocrates' particular intimacy with Plato is well known. He not only accompanied Plato on his trip to Sicily, but when the cruel tyrant Dionysius of Syracuse, who both loved and hated Plato at the same time, half-jokingly said that he might chop off his head, Xenocrates, himself probably dead serious, indicated to Dionysius that he would have to cut his own off first (Diogenes Laertius, IV, 11).

It is with this Xenocrates that Aristotle left the Academy after Plato's death.

## Some Doubts Concerning Aristotle's Departure from the Academy

The account we have given of Aristotle's departure from the Academy has been the most popular version since antiquity. But contemporary scholars have expressed other views as well which we deem necessary to mention although these views cannot be held to have been strictly proven.

If one considers that Aristotle left the Academy merely on account of differences with Plato, one is faced with the question of why he did not do so earlier. After all, works such as *On the Good* and *On the Ideas*, which harshly attack Plato, were written back in the mid-fifties. Therefore it would have been much more fitting for Aristotle to have left the Academy around 357-355 BC. True, one Syrian biography of Aristotle claims that he left the Academy before Plato's death, while Diogenes Laertius (V, 2) and Eusebius of Caeseria (*Preparatio Evangelica* XV, 2, 5) provide similar accounts. It is important to keep in mind that Plato allowed great variety of opinion among his students and in addition valued Aristotle for his enormous philosophical abilities even though Aristotle differed with him on many points. Speusippus' appointment as head of the school after Plato's death could also hardly have been the reason for Aristotle's departure, as some claim. Speusippus became the head of the Academy not so much through Plato's will and testament as through the inheritance laws of the time according to which the deceased's property was passed on to the closest male relative. And Plato had no children. Moreover, it is reported (albeit solely in a Syrian biography of Aristotle) that the ailing Speusippus wrote Aristotle a letter requesting him to return to the Academy and even become its head. The difference in views between Plato and Aristotle was hardly of decisive importance here. (As we have said, the liberal-minded Plato in general admitted heterogeneous opinions within his school. Note that Arcesilaus and Carneades, the next directors of the Academy after Speusippus and Xenocrates, established a new trend, scepticism, which they quite cleverly derived from Plato's own philosophy.) Finally, Speusippus soon died (339/8 BC), but even after his death Aristotle did not return to the Academy.

The most important point, which historians of Greek philosophy sometimes overlook, is that although Aristotle was a pure Greek, he harbored pro-Macedonian sympathies which never left him even when he entertained hostile feelings toward Macedonians, be these the kings Philip and Alexander. It is not at all surprising that in some important respects Aristotle inclined toward Macedonia. The famous orator and politician Aeschines (389-314 BC) was also a Greek who sympathized with Macedonia. To harbor such sentiments it was not at all necessary to have been born near the Macedonian border, although Stagira's territorial proximity to the Macedonian state might of course have been of some significance in the development of Aristotle's pro-Macedonian sympathies. Philip's razing of the Greek city of Olynthus in the summer of 348 BC stimulated a new wave of animosity toward the Macedonian king in Athens. But in the eyes of the Athenians Aristotle was an alien from Macedonia linked with the Macedonian king and incapable of assuming the right attitude to the destruction of Olynthus. In 306 BC the orator Demochares, son of Demosthenes' sister, who was subsequently exiled from Athens but who on his return gave substantial help to his native town on many occasions, said in his speech on a decree banishing philosophers from Athens that one of the former philosophers, specifically Aristotle, had actually denounced to Philip elements hostile to the king in Olynthus. But even Stagira, Aristotle's native town, was destroyed in 349 BC (Aristotle's parents had already died by then), and in 349/8 BC Philip instigated a rebellion against Athens on the island of Euboea where Aristotle's mother came from.

Therefore it was impossible for Aristotle to live either on Euboea or in Macedonia itself. If he did indeed go to Macedonia, it was only for a very short time. And the place he did travel to (as every one of the sources say) was the city of Atarneus in Asia Minor, to visit one of Plato's disciples, Hermeias. Hermeias himself was also accused of a secret deal with Philip against the Persians when they advanced close to his dominions, so that here, too, one can surmise pro-Macedonian sympathies on Aristotle's part.

In other words, the suggestion arises that Aristotle left the Academy (probably at the end of the summer of 348 BC) not at all on account of philosophical differences with Plato but, more likely, even before the latter's death, on account of the anti-Macedonian sentiment in Athens, which indeed kept on gathering head all over Greece. Much later, before his death, Aristotle wrote Antipater, Alexander's lieutenant in Greece, that strangers in Athens were forbidden things that citizens were allowed, and that it was dangerous in general for a Macedonian to live in Athens.

If one takes all such information seriously, then the political motivation of Aristotle's departure from the Academy becomes more than likely. Such a motivation is appealing if only because it projects a picture of Aristotle not as a retiring philosopher devoted solely to abstract argumentation but as a very energetic and even impassioned man, a direct participant in the turbulent political events of the

time. Aristotle did not have to choose between solitary sit-
ting in his quiet study and direct participation in the in-
tense political life of the day—although more often than
not philosophers face choices of this sort when they must
give preference to either secluded reflection or open social and political struggle. But Aristotle was a philosopher
who could not abandon his scholarly pursuits once and for
all and hurl himself into social and political life. Philosophy and practical life were one and the same for him.
That is why in the final analysis not even the motivation of
his departure from the Academy is important to us, but
the very fact of his emergence from solitude onto the
broad track of public life, which opened as yet unexplored
prospects before him.

### NOTES

[1]Diogenes Laertius, *Lives of Eminent Philosophers*, I: 381.
[2]"The Works of Aristotle", Vol. I, *Great Books of the Western World*,
Encyclopaedia Britannica, Inc., Chicago, 1952, 8: 506-08, 508-11, 514-16,
521-22.
[3]"The Works of Aristotle", Vol. II, *Great Books of the Western World*,
9: 341.
[4]Ibid., p. 594.

# III

# Aristotle's Literary and Philosophical Activity
## at the Academy

We consider it necessary to dwell on Aristotle's literary and philosophical activities while he was at Plato's Academy. The truth is that, except, of course, in narrowly specialized studies, scholars hardly touch on his work during this period. The reason is clear. Aristotle wrote such a mass of profound philosophical works which have been preserved that it requires an enormous amount of time merely to somehow master these. Aristotle's literary writings during the Academy period have reached us only in the form of individual fragments, the study and reconstruction of which by philologists is an extremely difficult task. This early period of Aristotle's creative work has been examined in studies by Werner Jaeger (1912, 1955), Paul Gohlke (1955), Ingmar Dühring (1957), Willy Theiler (1958), Otto Gigon (1958) and Anton Hermann Chroust (1973).

It is worth touching on these early works of Aristotle if only because everyone would naturally like to know how it was that Plato's nearest disciple moved on in other philosophical directions, how this shift occurred and what, properly speaking, is the difference between Aristotle and Plato, of which everyone speaks in various ways.

Aristotle could not immediately have become an adversary of Plato, otherwise there would have been no sense in his living at the Academy for nearly twenty years. Aristotle's divergence from Plato hardly came about all at once; it was gradual in the making. In view of the lack of precise chronological data it is uncertain whether the definitive break occurred while he was still at the Academy and whether it was definitive. It seems to us quite understandable that the young Aristotle should worship his teacher, at least in his first few years at the Academy. Therefore, out of the great many titles of works written by

Aristotle while at the Academy we shall first discuss those which are still rather naive philosophically and basically reiterate Plato's doctrines, and then turn to works in which he begins to diverge from Plato.

## The Dialogue and the Monologue Treatise

In the early days of his literary career Aristotle, following Plato's example, began by writing philosophical dialogues. Later on he gave up writing dialogues, and his scholarly works are essentially a concise exposition of his lectures and studies.

Plato was inclined to write metaphorically. He drew pleasure from showing people engaged in the process of philosophizing and discovering the truth rather than from systematically expounding his own teaching. Besides he viewed philosophy itself not as a realm of theoretical probings but as the reconstruction of all elements of being in the most general form.

But in the development of Plato's writing style one can single out a series of late dialogues in which his exposition had a more systematic and analytically abstract character. This discrepancy between the philosophical and artistic sides of his work is clearly manifested in his dialogue *Theaetetus,* where for the first time his interest in the method of philosophical meditation triumphed over his artistic aspirations. To a significant extent this dialogue already approaches a critical treatise.

In the *Sophist* and *Politicus, Timaeus* and *Philebus* it is even more evident that the dialogue form had become a special stylistic device for Plato with no longer any hint of artisticalness and dramatism. Socrates, the main figure in Plato's dialogues, was reduced to a secondary role after the *Sophist* and does not appear at all in the *Laws,* Plato's last piece.

Thus the urge to classify the subtlest twists of thought which prevailed in Plato's late period, a method which he called dialectics, entirely squeezed out artistic and dramatic features from his dialogues. The complete disappearance of his classical dialogue form was only a question of time, as its living roots had withered away. This is the very period when the young Aristotle appeared on the scene.

At the time everybody at the Academy wrote dialogues, but Aristotle wrote more than anybody else. The influence of his teacher was of course a factor here. But the clearer it became that Plato and his compositions were unique in their greatness, the more his students realized the need for new forms of investigations. They searched out these new forms primarily in the area of lectures. But Plato and Aristotle's inner closeness explains why Aristotle began with dialogues.

Aristotle can be considered the creator of a new form in which to a certain degree he revived the classical dialogue style on the basis of his experience of life at the Academy, abounding in philosophical arguments, exchanges of opinions and scholarly conversations. But to a large extent the personal element played only a subordinate part in these dialogues, and basically they were reminiscent of Plato's later dialogues. Aristotle did not at all destroy the dialogue structure as literary historians often claim, but actively participated in creating a new, post-dialogue form, the necessity for which was clear even to Plato.

Nevertheless, *Eudemus, or On the Soul* and *On Rhetoric, or Grylus*, are highly reminiscent of such early dialogues of Plato as *Phaedo* or *Gorgias*. The Socratic manner of conversing in the form of questions and answers is still clearly visible in *Eudemus* (fragment 44). In other dialogues, such as the *Politicus* and *On Philosophy*, which consisted of two or three books, Aristotle, as far as we can infer from individual fragments (8-9, 78), probably expounded his subject matter directly. The steps in the transition from a Socratic manner (still possible in *Eudemus*) to an almost strictly monologic exposition are the outward expression of Aristotle's own inner philosophical development.

There are often very evident parallels between his dialogues and dialogues of Plato. Thus, *Eudemus* goes back to *Phaedo*, *Grylus* to *Gorgias*, *On Justice* to the *Republic*. The *Sophist, Politicus, Symposium* and *Menexenus* also derive from the Platonic dialogues of the same names. In the non-dialogic *Protrepticus* one can trace the admonitory

39

section of Plato's *Euthydemus* right down to literal correspondences. It is possible that Plato served as an interlocutor in Aristotle's dialogues as Socrates did in Plato's. Aristotle's style here is distinctively pure and clear, for he felt that the power of scientific knowledge should affect one's language, too. At the same time *Eudemus* contains a retelling of the myth of Midas and frequent comparisons along Platonic models.

Generally speaking the style of Aristotle's early works gave pleasure to many people, as testified by the ancients, for example the cynic philosopher Crates of Thebes, who read Aristotle's *Protrepticus* with the cobbler Philiscus in his workshop (fragment 50). Aristotle's dialogues caught the interest of the stoics Zeno of Citium, Chrysippus, Cleanthes, and subsequently, of Cicero, Philo of Alexandria and Saint Augustine (354-430 AD). The latter became acquainted with *Protrepticus* through Cicero's dialogue *Hortensius*.[1] We can find echoes of Aristotle's early works still later, in the sixth-century philosopher Boethius. Of course for all their merits Aristotle's dialogues even in antiquity were never placed on a par with Plato's, although in the Hellenistic period of late antiquity they perhaps had an even greater significance.

But now we must ask: what was the relation between teacher and pupil in the area of pure philosophy? Unfortunately at the time of Andronicus of Rhodes, who studied Aristotle's works in Rome in the first century BC, the dialogues of the young Aristotle had been pushed into the background by a newly aroused interest in his systematic works, which had been neglected for a long time. The Peripatetic scholars[2], followers of Aristotle's school, turned to these works and began to study them intensively. The strict Peripatetic Alexander of Aphrodisias (second and third centuries AD) felt that in his dialogues Aristotle merely reported the opinions of other philosophers, and his own opinion had to be looked for in his maturer works. Many of Aristotle's dialogues were considered to be something esoteric, i.e., written in an outwardly popular format contrary to his true teachings outlined in treatises for a narrow circle of readers. Yet from the comments of Plutarch (first century AD) and Proclus (fifth century AD) it is evident that the content of Aristotle's earliest dialogues was very similar to that of his late critical writings (fragment 8).[3] Hence we can conclude either that Aristotle's departure from Platonism can be dated from the Academy period, or that his dialogues have a later origin.

On the basis of this testimony a number of specialists have categorically denied any traces of Plato's philosophy in Aristotle's dialogues. At the same time the dialogues form a unified whole that clearly contrasts with all Aristotle's other works.

## Early Rhetorical Concerns

Before we turn to Aristotle's main works from the Academy period, we must touch on a most interesting point, which, although attested by only a few sources, nevertheless contributes enormously to Aristotle's characterization, in our opinion. This circumstance is that in the first years of his stay at the Academy Aristotle gave a whole long lecture course on rhetoric. We have already remarked on the fact that Aristotle was concerned with rhetoric all his life. He gave lectures on rhetoric before his departure from the Academy in 347 BC and later after his return to Athens in 335 BC he resumed giving these lectures in the Lyceum which he founded.[4] The Epicurean philosopher Philodemus of Gadara (first century BC) even reproached Aristotle for having spent too much time on such an external affair as rhetoric and devoted much less attention to philosophy. This is of course not true. Rhetoric for Aristotle was only the packaging for philosophy and was fully thought out on a philosophical plane. It is probably in his view of the purposes of rhetoric that Aristotle differed with the famous Isocrates, whose school he left very early. Perhaps one should regard the young Aristotle's lectures on rhetoric at the Academy as being a symbol of the difference between the two schools, Isocrates' and Plato's, and only serving to strengthen Plato's Academy in the eyes of society. To have an exact notion of the direction in which Aristotle's rhetorical theory was developing when he was still at the Academy, one need only read the significant pages of Plato's *Phaedrus* (268a-272e).[5] Here Plato sharply criticized empty eloquence and defended rhetoric as a method for getting to

41

know the human soul and, for the orator, to influence human souls. Under Isocrates Aristotle undoubtedly learned to use words elegantly, but added to this skill profound philosophical content, initially drawn from none other than Plato. True, today many people find it very hard to believe in the brilliance and elegance of Aristotle's speech.

The texts of Aristotle that have reached us are extremely difficult and poorly intelligible because of the heaping up of complex and most subtle logical arguments. But one must remember that most of Aristotle's works have come down to us in the form of notes taken by his listeners and have suffered a multitude of distortions over the centuries at the hands of scribes, commentators and readers. In any case, Aristotle's very late work *Rhetoric* still astounds us today with his profound knowledge of life situations and his rare ability to grasp and find a way out of them. Therefore the universal opinion of Aristotle's works as obscure, unreadable and sometimes disconnected is utterly erroneous. But one can prove the mistakenness of this view only by analyzing certain very fine arguments of Aristotle. We shall limit ourselves to citing the sentiments of a few ancient writers on this subject.

In his treatise *De Oratore,* Cicero writes: "Accordingly when Aristotle observed that Isocrates succeeded in obtaining a distinguished set of pupils by means of abandoning legal and political subjects and devoting his discourses to empty elegance of style, he himself suddenly altered almost the whole of his own system of training, and quoted a line from *Philoctetes* [the tragedy by Sophocles] with a slight modification; the hero in the tragedy said that it was a disgrace for him to keep silent and suffer Barbarians to speak, but Aristotle put it 'suffer Isocrates to speak'; and consequently he put the whole of his system of philosophy in a polished and brilliant form, and linked the scientific study of facts with practice in style. Nor indeed did this escape the notice of that extremely sagacious monarch Philip, who summoned Aristotle to be the tutor of his son Alexander, and to impart to him the principles both of conduct and of oratory."[6]

In another treatise of his, entitled *Orator,* Cicero discourses as follows: "Aristotle trained young men in this,

42

not for the philosophical manner of subtle discussion, but for the fluent style of the rhetorician, so that they might be able to uphold either side of the question in copious and elegant language" (XIV, 46).[7] In the same treatise Cicero admonishes orators as follows: "The orator will treat these topics, not in the fashion of the Peripatetics — to them belongs a graceful method of philosophical discussion which as a matter of fact goes back to Aristotle — but with somewhat greater vigor" (XXXVI, 127). Here, too, we read: "But who ever exceeded Aristotle in learning or in acumen, in originality of thought or in subtlety of dialectic? Who again was a more violent opponent of Isocrates?" (LI, 172). Cicero's judgment in the *Tusculan Disputations* is also important: "But just as Aristotle, a man of supreme genius, knowledge and fertility of speech, under the stimulus of the fame of the rhetorician Isocrates, began like him to teach the young to speak and combine wisdom with eloquence, similarly it is my design not to lay aside my early devotion to the art of expression" (I, 4, 7).[8] Quintilian, from whom we learn of Aristotle's lectures on rhetoric at the Academy, says approximately the same thing as Cicero.[9]

Thus the ancients, and moreover such an authority as Cicero, had a definite opinion as to Aristotle's graceful style and his involvement with rhetoric throughout his life. Later on Aristotle departed from Plato, but he never abandoned rhetoric.

### Aristotle's Earliest Dialogues

One of Aristotle's earliest and still very naive writings from the Academy period is entitled *Magian* (fragments 32-36). Aristotle's authorship of this work is somewhat questionable, as others are also named as its authors. This dialogue opposes Hellenic and Barbarian philosophy. Of the Barbarian philosophers he takes the famous Persian sage Zoroaster, who in his religious thinking had already departed from naive spontaneity and made wide use of philosophical argumentation. Diogenes Laertius' general remark on the Persian magi is typical: "With the art of magic they were wholly unacquainted, according to Aristotle in his *Magicus*" (I, 8). The magi engaged in divination, soothsaying, sacrificing and writing philosophical treatises.

This point alone is very characteristic of Aristotle, who subsequently became famous as a champion of theoretical philosophic thinking and scientific criticism.

Let us now examine what else we know concerning Aristotle's writings at the Academy. Judging from the few lines that have been preserved in fragment 49, one can say that for Aristotle, as for Plato, the most important thing in all of existence was what they both called mind. But this is not at all the mind of an individual person or even of some divinity, but simply the totality of all regularities that exist in the world. Here Aristotle does not yet set forth the developed doctrine of the mind which is found in book XII of his *Metaphysics*, and the mind here is not yet so absolute as not to allow of anything else that is higher than the mind; it is also not so independent as to exclude all individual subjective moods and states. These are the noteworthy elements we find in the still relatively immature period of Aristotle's philosophy. The late commentator Simplicius (527-565 AD) wrote that Aristotle evidently assumed something above mind and essence because at the end of his book on prayer he literally said that God was either Mind or something beyond Mind.

The following two fragments apparently also date from this early period. The philosopher Seneca (first century AD) praises Aristotle for saying that we must be most timid, i.e., reverential, where the gods are concerned, while the Greek author Synesius of the fourth and fifth centuries AD reports that Aristotle believed people were perfected not through training but through experience and a certain spiritual disposition (fragment 15).

It is quite evident that for the time being Aristotle remained well within the sphere of Plato's ideas. But it is already apparent that Aristotle's discourse is not the purely formal one of a pupil but attests to the young man's great depth and freshness of feeling. To an even greater extent, perhaps, this is true of another dialogue from the Academy period, entitled *Eudemus, or On the Soul*.

44

## The Dialogue *Eudemus, or On the Soul.*

The date of the composition of *Eudemus* (fragments 37-48) is largely determined by the very content of this dialogue. The circumstances which led to Aristotle's writing of this piece are known to us from Cicero. Eudemus, a pupil of Plato's, exiled from his native Cyprus, became gravely ill while travelling through Thessaly. The doctors in the city of Pherae, where Eudemus lay sick, considered his case hopeless. And then Eudemus had a dream of a beautiful youth who promised that he would soon recover, that a little later Alexander, the tyrant of Pherae, would die, and that at the end of five years Eudemus would return to his homeland. In the dialogue's exordium Aristotle described how the first and second predictions had come true: Eudemus recovered, and the tyrant was soon killed by his wife's brothers (359 BC). It must be noted that the third prediction was not fulfilled: Eudemus joined a party planning the return to his country of Plato's friend and pupil Dion of Syracuse (many members of the Academy belonged to this party) and died in battle outside the walls of Syracuse in 354 BC, exactly five years after his dream. At the Academy the prediction was interpreted to have meant not the earthly but the eternal spiritual homeland of the soul.

The exordium to the dialogue, where these events are recounted, is dedicated to the memory of Eudemus. In Aristotle's mind, the story of the dream was supposed to confirm Plato's doctrine of the unearthly origin of the soul and its future return to its homeland. Such an introduction gave occasion to a conversation on the immortality of the soul. In this dialogue of the young Aristotle the world of Plato's *Phaedo* was reborn: the image of the temporary exile of the soul and its bondage in the fetters of the body is contained in the story of the fugitive banished from his fatherland.

Like Plato, Aristotle is in this case opposing those who deny the immortality of the soul. He refutes the opinion that the soul is only a harmony of the body, i.e., although not merely a sum of material particles, still something resulting from their proper combination. Aristotle cites two arguments against this view.

Aristotle's first argument can be summarized as follows. There can be no harmony, i.e., a certain ordered combination of individual parts, if these parts themselves do not exist. But these parts may be disordered and discordant. Consequently, for them to be ordered they themselves are not sufficient, and there must be some other essence besides, different from them but ordering them. Thus harmony is a certain condition or quality of a specific essence, opposed to another, contrary condition or quality. But the soul cannot stand in opposition to something in the way that harmony can be opposed to disharmony. Consequently, the soul is not a property of some essence, but essence itself. We see that Aristotle is already quite clearly distinguishing the essence of an object from its qualities, a distinction which will later play a big role in his *Categories*.

It must be said that Aristotle's proof is simpler than Plato's in the *Phaedo*. Plato also comes to the conclusion that harmony can be a property of the soul, but can in no way be the soul itself. Aristotle's proof, which can be considered a slight adaptation of Plato's, clearly shows Plato's influence on him as a logician. According to Aristotle, essence (or substance) cannot be that which it is, to a greater or lesser degree. Hence it followed for Plato and Aristotle that not the soul but its properties, such as harmony, virtue and so on, could change to varying degrees. Aristotle, already possessed of Plato's proof, merely gave a somewhat simpler expression to the same idea, from which he also drew his second proof.

Opposed to the harmony of the body is its disharmony. But this is sickness, weakness and ugliness. Then harmony is health, strength and beauty. The soul is none of these. For even Homer's ugly warrior Thersites had a soul. Therefore the soul is not harmony.

This second proof flows directly from Plato's theory of man and his division of human virtues insofar as they pertain to the soul or the body. Plato's virtues had corresponding opposites. If the virtues rested on harmony (symmetry), then their contraries were founded on disharmony (asymmetry). Plato borrowed the explanation of weakness or sickness as an asymmetry in the body's particles from the medicine of his day, which is undoubtedly also the source of his science of ethics as therapy of the soul.

This theory clarifies Aristotle's train of thought: if harmony is the foundation of corporeal virtues, then the soul cannot of course be harmony.

Thus in his proofs Aristotle follows Plato, or more precisely, his doctrine of the soul, in almost every respect. In his subsequent works Aristotle took an intermediate position between the ones he defended and criticized in *Eudemus*: the soul is inseparable from the body and, consequently, mortal, although at the same time it is the formative principle of any organism. It is noteworthy that in *Eudemus* the soul is called "a certain idea" (*eidos ti*), and not "the idea of something" (*eidos tinos*). This wording emphasizes the independent and utterly irreducible character of the soul, and does so not in a Platonic but in a new manner.

The hidden meaning in the philosophical depths of *Eudemus* is glimpsed in the story of King Midas and Silenus, retold in Platonic terms. Asked by the king what the highest good is, Silenus describes the misfortune and suffering that are the lot of humans. It is utterly impossible, Aristotle reasons, for the children of men to partake in the highest good; they can never be privy to the nature of the best. For the greatest good for all is not to be born. But if they have been born, the best thing, and this is possible for people, is to die as soon as possible. The meaning of this passage (fragment 44) is that the death of the body frees the soul for eternal life, for immutable Being.

The most Platonic aspect of the dialogue is the doctrine of the immortality of the soul, which also goes back to the *Phaedo*. Although later in his psychology Aristotle repudiated the theory of the immortality of the soul, in *Eudemus* he accepts it completely. As for the psychological problem of the existence of consciousness after death, it was presented here for the first time and solved also by Platonic means. Life outside the body is the normal condition of the soul; life in the body is a grave illness. One's forgetting of the sights of one's former life is explained by a break in the continuity of consciousness and memory. This reasoning is based on the Platonic idea that human knowledge is only a recollection of something seen in former life.

*Eudemus* contains a great many Platonic elements and direct reminiscences, but the closed circle of argumentation in the dialogue lacks the final link—the Ideas as they appear in Plato's *Phaedo*. Yet all the other elements of the doctrine of the soul urgently require the theory of the Ideas, as Plato himself had noted. And since Aristotle subsequently relinquished the purely Platonic doctrine of the Ideas, he also gave up Plato's theory of recollection.

Analysis of the fragments of *Eudemus* shows that Aristotle is quite independent in the logic of his argumentations and proofs, although ideologically he still depends on Plato. The soul, according to Aristotle here, is immortal, as it is for Plato. But Aristotle's theory of the immortality of the soul does not rest directly on an unconditional acknowledgment of the eternal Idea of the soul, but follows from purely logical proofs. Aristotle is trying to say that for the attributes of such and such an object to exist the object itself must first be recognized. Therefore, if various manifestations, various abilities and states of the soul exist, affirmations of this sort are possible only if the soul is admitted to exist in itself. But this means that the soul considered in itself does not contain any attributes or properties, and consequently does not alter in time. That is why it is eternal and immortal.

Let us now turn to the *Protrepticus*.

## Protrepticus, or Exhortation

*Protrepticus*[10] (fragments 50-61) holds as meaningful a place among Aristotle's early works as *Eudemus*. But the exact date of its composition, as well as its form and content, have not yet been sufficiently elucidated.

*Protrepticus* is exceptional among Aristotle's early works. It is addressed to Themison of Cyprus. Although almost nothing is known of this insignificant ruler, from Isocrates' panegyric to Evagoras and his epistle to Nicocles, also a *protrepticus*, one can by analogy form some idea of Themison as an enlightened man who was interested in philosophy. In any event, there is scarcely any doubt that Aristotle's epistle was composed in accordance with the goals of the political activities that were being extensively conducted by the Academy at the time.

The exordium to the *Protrepticus* is an address to Themison, who as a result of his power and authority is said to be destined to be a philosopher. This was hardly flattery, since Themison evidently was supposed to put into practice the Academy's teachings on the state and the philosopher-king.

The form of the work is closely linked to its edifying content, and goes back to the sophists, who replaced the verse admonitions that had been known since the poet Hesiod's day with exhortations in prose. One can conclude on the basis of later *protreptici* that they bear a similarity to the edifying speeches of the Hellenistic period, which later gave birth to the Christian epistles and sermons.

But Aristotle's *Protrepticus* can best be compared with Isocrates' works. Aristotle proclaims a new, Platonic ideal of a ruler engaged in philosophy and leading a contemplative life.

Should man philosophize, asks Aristotle. Even if one rejects philosophizing, one will need to resort to philosophizing to argue this refusal. Consequently, philosophizing is necessary in any case. Thus Aristotle heightened the effect of the old admonitory devices with the help of logical inferences. *Protrepticus* demonstrates the Academy's penchant for rhetorical methods. But Aristotle spurns the trivial tenets adhered to by Isocrates and his circle, who felt that the art of rhetoric alone and a healthy life style were quite sufficient for human happiness, and that it was not in the least obligatory to engage in pure philosophizing. It is significant that the unknown author of the *Consolatio ad Demonicum*, which is strikingly polemical and anti-Platonic in character, most likely belonged to Isocrates' school. The main idea in the exordium to this work is that those who try to instruct young people with the help of purely philosophical reasoning not only do not assist their moral improvement but face them with troublesome tasks as well. It is possible that Aristotle himself was counted among such preceptors. A comparison of certain passages in both works also confirms that the anonymous *Consolatio* was most probably a response to Aristotle's work.

After painstaking philological investigations it was established already over a century ago that considerable fragments of Aristotle's piece are contained in the *Protrepticus* of the fourth-century AD neo-Platonic philosopher Iamblichus, where the pronouncements of various philosophers, including Plato, were gathered for homiletic purposes. The *Protrepticus* was cited as proof of Aristotle's adherence to Platonism. The major portion of Iamblichus' *Protrepticus* consists of excerpts from Plato's dialogues. But approximately half-way through, these extracts are interrupted by quotations from Aristotle's *Protrepticus*.

The use of Aristotle's *Protrepticus* by such philosophers of late antiquity as Cicero, Saint Augustine, Proclus and Boethius assisted in the identification of citations from it. The only question is whether Iamblichus integrally quoted these passages from Aristotle or whether he himself constructed proofs on the basis of Aristotle's material. First of all it must be noted that whereas the extracts from Plato are connected externally and often haphazardly, the theses borrowed from Aristotle are internally connected. But all that can be concluded for sure from this fact is a similarity between Aristotle's and Iamblichus' methods of constructing proofs. Most probably Iamblichus merely used material from Aristotle (though in a very thorough-going way), and one can scarcely speak of a strictly Aristotelian composition here, even if it is beyond doubt that it was Aristotle's ideas that formed the basis of many of Iamblichus' arguments. Particularly rich in borrowings is Chapter Seven, where a great many arguments can be qualified as coming directly from Aristotle, as is confirmed by also comparing them with some passages from the *Metaphysics* dealing with strict scientific knowledge, although in the *Metaphysics* these ideas appear only in the introduction. There are quite a few excerpts from Aristotle in other chapters of Iamblichus' *Protrepticus* as well, for instance in the ninth, tenth, eleventh and twelfth. Taken together all these references allow one to reconstruct to some extent the content and philosophical tendency of Aristotle's own *Protrepticus*.

The point and meaning of Aristotle's *Protrepticus* is that in it he does not examine particular issues but deals with the most general problem – the essence of philosophy, its right to existence and its significance for human life in general, and, more specifically, it deals with the essence of the Platonic ideal of human life and the way to achieve it, namely, Plato's philosophy.

It is no accident that Aristotle, representing the younger generation of Academy students, should have made an attempt to justify Plato's ideal of life to the outer world, since the opposition between theory and practice was felt particularly keenly by this generation.

All of Socrates' philosophy, and then Plato's, sprang from practical experience and the necessities of life, emerging into a purely theoretical sphere only in its highest manifestation – and in the doctrine of the Ideas. Socrates' doctrine of the cognition of virtue demanded the primacy of creative reason, contemplating pure being and creating life upon this basis. A deserving and virtuous life could therefore consist only in contemplating the highest truth. The younger generation of Academicians, nurtured on this truth, nevertheless had to raise anew the issue of the value of the "contemplative life" – and to search for it in the inner, pure happiness of cognition and the union of reason and eternity. Thus Plato's ideal was reexamined by his pupils and in the process acquired a contemplatively religious character.

*Phronesis*, the concept which most fully expressed such an ideal, was the focus of Aristotle's attention. This concept can be defined as the creative cognition of the highest good, which becomes accessible thanks to the inner contemplation of pure being; as a result, the soul's inner capabilities account for a person's deserving actions and true knowledge. This is how *phronesis*, or the creative intellect, was understood by Socrates and his followers up to Aristotle's time. In his *Protrepticus* Aristotle still assumes a Platonic position, i.e., he understands *phronesis* as pure theoretical reason. A secondary meaning of the term indicating a separate area of knowledge is almost not encountered in the *Protrepticus*. Here *phronesis* is Mind, the divine element in us, a capability of the soul rising high above all other capabilities, precisely as the term is used in Plato's dialogues *Timaeus, Philebus* or his *Laws*.

In Aristotle's later works, such as the *Metaphysics* and *Nicomachean Ethics,* this conception of *phronesis* as intellect is no longer encountered. Here the concept is endowed with a pre-Platonic, in other words purely practical meaning, and is sharply distinguished from the sphere of the mind. In this sense *phronesis* exists even in animals, and consists not in reflection on general things and concepts but simply in observation of particular things, and consequently *phronesis* is neither the most valuable part of knowledge nor any kind of science at all (*Nicomachean Ethics* VI, 7, 8). Thus Aristotle quite obviously gave up the tenets of his *Protrepticus* later on.

However, underlying these changes in terminology are modifications in Aristotle's views of metaphysics and ethics. It follows that when he was writing the *Protrepticus* Aristotle held a different position: he recognized the theory of Ideas and, consequently, Plato's metaphysics. In no other work apart from the *Protrepticus* does Aristotle accept the division of philosophy into dialectics, physics (theory of nature) and ethics, as was the practice at Plato's Academy. Likewise ethics is presented here as Plato's doctrine of the four virtues and is understood as a kind of knowledge related to the exact sciences, such as geometry. Politics is also seen as exact and purely theoretical knowledge.

This "mathematical" nature of ethics and politics sharply contradicts what Aristotle wrote in his later works, where he came out against strict exactitude in the methodology of these disciplines and compared them rather to rhetoric than to mathematics (*Nicomachean Ethics* I, 1). Later Aristotle also rejected the Platonic ideal of the philosopher-king, asserting that it was not at all necessary for a ruler to philosophize, but it was sufficient for him merely to listen to the advice of a wise man (fragment 647). Aristotle apparently arrived at this conviction during Alexander the Great's campaign in Asia.

The need to raise philosophy to the level of exact science is also reflected in the interpretation of relations between empirical science, founded on experiment, and strict theoretical science in the *Protrepticus*. When the opponent of philosophy in *Protrepticus* proclaims that theory is harmful because it only hinders practice, we expect that Aristotle (although the corresponding fragment has not been preserved, the tendency of his thinking can be reconstructed) will respond in the spirit of late Platonism, i.e., elevate precise philosophical knowledge of the most general concepts above all particular sciences, and give preference to the purity and precision of theory over practical usefulness. The philosopher, in contrast to those involved in individual sciences and in the arts, contemplates the highest principles and imitates precision itself; he views the things themselves, nature and truth themselves, and not their imperfect likenesses perceptible to the senses. The meaning of this discussion is without a doubt purely Platonic and goes back to the doctrine of Ideas in book IX of the *Republic* (599a, 600e, 602c, 603a, 605b).[11]

Similar arguments appear several times in Aristotle's *Protrepticus*. The aim of human existence is knowledge, therefore it is absurd to ask what kind of knowledge is good in itself. Perfect and unhindered activity contains pleasure within itself, therefore only philosophers are capable of fully enjoying life (fragment 61). As Aristotle says in fragment 52 of this work, the acquisition of wisdom affords enjoyment. All people feel at home in philosophy and strive to abandon all other cares and spend their whole lives studying it. Philosophers need neither tools nor a specially equipped place for their work: wherever in the world anyone may ponder, he is everywhere surrounded by the presence of truth.

Of great significance in the *Protrepticus* is the examination of the elements of being (*stoicheia*), of which each preceding one is more important than the following. Among these in fragment 52 are listed numbers, lines, planes and bodies. Later the mature Aristotle would object to this classification in his *Metaphysics* (V, 8; XIV, 3), or rather, indicate that it was a Platonic view.

From the preceding summary one can conclude that at the time he was writing the *Protrepticus* Aristotle accepted the doctrine of the Ideas and although he recognized the difficulties connected with it, nevertheless he did not consider them sufficient grounds to reject the whole theory. He did so later in his works *On Philosophy* and *Metaphysics* after Plato's death.

The views in the *Protrepticus*, as in Plato's late dialogues, unquestionably are in keeping with the general ideal of a pure and strict mathematized science which had arisen in the Academy environment. Plato's students began to seek the "contemplative life" this ideal required in more ancient philosophers: Pythagoras, Anaxagoras and Parmenides. At the same time their interest in the figure of Socrates gradually faded because the Academy was irreversibly moving away from the Socratic style of life and thinking. In any event, the theoretical philosophy of the *Protrepticus* has nothing in common with the Socratic type and regards Pythagoras as the forefather of Platonic philosophy. The Pythagorean character of Platonism is commented upon even in the first book of the *Metaphysics* (I, 6). This comment cannot be considered an attempt to somehow belittle Plato's importance, for the view was officially accepted at the Academy, where Pythagoras was also professed to be the originator of the "contemplative life". In the *Protrepticus* he appears as the "contemplator" (*theoros*) of everything there is in the world.

Finally, to a somewhat greater extent than the abstract arguments of *Eudemus*, the *Protrepticus* reveals for us the personality of Aristotle, his moral and religious temper. The life of the body, according to Aristotle here, is the death of the soul, while the death of the body is the resurrection of the soul to a higher life. The life of the philosopher should be a constant preparation for corporeal death, for the liberation of the soul. For its sufferings in the fetters of the body are like the sufferings of the living people the Etruscan pirates would bind to corpses. The *Protrepticus* warns against too great involvement in the life of the senses. One should turn to the truth, otherwise it is better to leave this world entirely. All else is empty words (fragment 61). At this time Aristotle undoubtedly felt this world of Platonic Ideas and allegories to be an integral part of his own self.

Aristotle's *Protrepticus* apparently occupies an intermediate position between pure Platonism and Aristotle's own later teachings. The realm of Ideas above the world is still admitted here in a definite and confident enough form insofar as the work advances the ancient teaching of the orphic philosophers on the transmigration of souls, or at least the necessity of liberating the immortal soul from the mortal body.[12] At the same time, however, Aristotle builds his conception of pure intellectual speculation with the help of terminology which, both as it is generally used in Greek and as it is applied by Plato, testifies to practical rather than speculative intelligence. Such is the case of the term *phronesis,* of which we spoke above. One must conjecture that Aristotle uses this term with an unconscious presentiment of the specifically practical bias pure speculation was to have for him.

### The Dialogue *On Philosophy*

The doctrine developed by Aristotle in his dialogue *On Philosophy* is patently un-Platonic in nature. To be sure, even here the un-Platonic conception does not at all bear the character of a flagrant repudiation and in many respects rests again on that same Plato. However, what is important are the main tendencies in this dialogue, the attempt to reform in some way or another Plato's strict theory of the Ideas.

Aristotle's departure from Athens can in no way be explained solely by a break with the Academy circle, although it is also quite clear that it was at this time that Aristotle first came out with open criticism of Plato. Hence it follows that the entire period between his departure from Athens in 347 BC and his founding of the Lyceum in 335 BC can be considered a transitional stage between Aristotle's initial unconditional acceptance of Plato and the second, crowning stage in his philosophical development.

It is during this middle period that the basic concepts of his own system were generated. The dialogue *On Philosophy,* which is sometimes listed among his earlier dialogues, should be placed at the center of his philosophical development during this period, for the philosophy and the form itself of the dialogue manifest transitional features, while its style, tendency and content allow this work to occupy a completely independent position among Aristotle's other compositions.

One can determine the time dialogue was written because it represents a first draft of Aristotle's critique of the theory of Ideas which was developed in Book I of his *Metaphysics.* The dialogue *On Philosophy* and Book I of the *Metaphysics* were therefore written close together in time and can both be dated to the years immediately following Plato's death.

The content of the dialogue is distinctly anti-Platonic and is primarily directed against the theory of the numerical conception of the Ideas, which had originated with Plato himself and not Speusippus, as was formerly believed. Apparently it is to this work that Plutarch and Proclus were referring when they reported that Aristotle criticized Plato not only in his treatises but in his dialogues as well. The title of the dialogue and the form of the preserved fragments attest to the more systematic character of this work compared to Aristotle's other dialogues. Aristotle and a defender of Platonic philosophy are conversing about philosophy. His interlocutor's arguments prompt Aristotle to plunge into a long discourse.

He begins with an historical sketch on the development of philosophy. He traces it from the time of the magi, turning next to an evaluation of Egyptian and Hellenic philosophers, and devoting considerable attention to the famous seven sages of Greece.[13] This strictly chronological account (from Aristotle's point of view) is not, however, of purely historical interest. Aristotle intends to demonstrate that people repeatedly discovered the very same truths. A similar idea lies behind his ascription of the saying "know thyself" not to one of the seven sages but to the Pythia of the temple at Delphi herself, from whom the sages borrowed this divine thought, which Socrates later interpreted anew.

Aristotle's idea is clear: all philosophical views recur many times in the course of the ages and at their origins are close to traditional folk beliefs.

Aristotle's special interest in the magi, and eastern thought in general, in this dialogue can be explained by the respect for oriental wisdom, particularly mathematics and astronomy, which in general characterized the Academy circle in the final period of Plato's life. Aristotle's research into the chronology of Zoroaster's life was preceded by analogous research on the part of the Platonists Eudoxūs, Hermodorus and Xanthus. But when Aristotle asserts that Zoroaster lived six thousand years before Plato[14], he is again emphasizing his belief in the natural periodic revival of ancient truths. Note that one of the earliest parts of the *Metaphysics* (XIII, 4) also mentions the magi and their dualistic teaching as precursors of Plato's dualism and theory of the good. Thus Aristotle showed Plato's organic connection with divine thought through the centuries, and Aristotle's whole theory of the cyclical succession of truths is nothing but Plato's doctrine of the periodicity of cosmic catastrophes adapted to the history of philosophy.

In this connection it must also be noted that although Aristotle criticizes Plato in the Second Book of the dialogue and develops his own theory in Book III, he has nevertheless not abandoned Platonism where cosmology is concerned, as is attested by the similarity of his conception of the gods to Plato's in the *Epinomis*, as well as by resemblances in terminology. Differences in particulars do not prevent Aristotle from following Plato's example in joining theology, or teachings about the gods, with astronomy. Aristotle's cosmos, embracing the sun, moon and stars, fully corresponds to Plato's cosmos in the dialogue *Timaeus*.

However, the heavens, for Aristotle, are no longer a reflection of the highest Idea, which embraces all the lesser ones. He has left aside the world of the Ideas, along with the demiurge who creates the material world modelled after the Ideas. The cosmos itself is now seen as the visible unity of the world and the constellations; it contains something divine. The stars are sentient beings endowed with a soul; they dwell in the cosmos in divine immutability and beauty. These are already Hellenistic conceptions current in late antiquity, but Plato was their source.

It must be said that there was also a place in such a cosmos for a motive force which, akin to an Idea and acting from the outside, gave meaning to and held together the unity of the cosmos. The notion of such an incorporeal mover is also purely Platonic. Aristotle merely transformed it into a supreme principle. At the same time, the stars in his cosmos were capable of spontaneous motion, a belief the philosopher later rejected.

Consequently, although Aristotle did wrestle with Plato, he still held to Platonic positions, and overcame his teacher not by refuting him outright but by imposing his own interpretation on Platonism.

The same can be said of the theological section of the dialogue *On Philosophy*. The times of naive faith had passed. Now it was necessary not only to recognize the presence of a god but to prove his existence as well. Aristotle created what much later, past antiquity, was given the name of philosophy of religion. In the dialogue *On Philosophy* he for the first time grounded the existence of a divinity in logical deductions. He says in fragment 16 that in every sphere where there is a series of steps, where there is a higher or a lower with respect to perfection, one can affirm that there necessarily exists absolute perfection as well. And because in that which exists there is a gradation of things of greater and lesser perfection, there is also an all-perfect being, and it can be considered divine. Here is the basis of a proof of a divine being which, in accordance with Aristotle's theory of nature, i.e., physics, is linked with an affirmation of expediency in nature itself. In nature there is a certain relationship of lower to higher, and this order was quite obvious or empirically evident to Aristotle.

In spite of all the new elements in this dialogue, on the whole Aristotle is following in the direction indicated by Plato. In this work Aristotle also points to the psychological bases of religion.[15] Again it was Plato who had first given philosophical form to the idea of the inner contemplation of the divinity. Aristotle applied this concept to the problem of the relationship between knowledge and faith. He sees inner concentration as the essence of any religious feeling. Priority here is accorded not to reason but to inner emotional experience.

Aristotle derives the inner knowledge of the divine from two sources: the sense of a certain daemonic force in one's soul, and one's contemplation of the starry heavens. This is none other than the religious consciousness of Plato's disciples given more articulate form by Aristotle and resting on a recognition of forces inaccessible to scientific cognition—a thought not at all in keeping with the mature Aristotle's scientific aspirations. Following Aristotle, the stoic philosophers viewed faith as a subjective emotional experience of the human soul and the result

58

of contemplating the objective existence of the eternal starry heavens. The renowned German philosopher Immanuel Kant expressed the same thought nearly two thousand years later, in the eighteenth century.

Aristotle was the first Greek who gazed on the real world through Plato's eyes. But he replaced the Ideas with contemplation of the shaped and ordered cosmos, thus expressing the aspirations of the Academic circle to link eastern astral theories with Greek religion.

To formulate Aristotle's new departure from Plato (which was not, however, entirely foreign to Plato himself), we would like to draw the reader's attention to fragment 16 especially. Here Aristotle says that both worse and better exist in the world. But if one can pass from worse to better, one can reach the very best as well. Today we would state the same idea more simply. If there is a natural series of numbers, i.e., moving from one to two, from two to three and so on, then the transition to an infinite number is also necessary. Hence any gradation of things in the world makes us pass on to a limit of such changes beyond which one can go no further. According to Aristotle, God is this infinity. Moreover, this infinity cannot become greater, since it already contains all that is greatest. Nor can it become lesser, since all the least is already contained in it; infinity minus one according to any mathematical textbook will still remain infinity. Likewise nothing can affect this infinity because it already embraces all that could affect it in one way or another. For the same reason it cannot become more beautiful or more ugly. For infinity itself already encompasses everything that could exist as a value of some kind.

This train of reasoning, generally speaking, can also be considered Platonic. But what is typical of Aristotle is that he proceeds not from top to bottom but, on the contrary, from the bottom up. Therefore his proof of divine infinity undoubtedly has an empirical character and is aimed not so much at grounding the existence of the cosmos on the recognition of a divinity as at presenting this divinity as the foundation of the cosmos itself, the principle of its orderliness. But even a sceptic, without using the word "God", would fully agree that there exists in the world a certain regularity, manifested from without, and could even formulate this universal regularity in precise mathematical terms. Of course there is much that is incomprehensible in Aristotle's discussion (the problems being compounded by fragmentation), since this is still the very beginning of his philosophical independence from Plato. But there are also many difficulties concealed here which Aristotle did not surmount to the end of his life and could hardly have overcome conclusively. In fragment 26 Cicero frankly reproaches Aristotle with great confusion in the thoughts expressed in this text. At one moment Aristotle speaks of Mind as an infinite universal regularity located outside the world, at another he says that the world is itself a god; then again this god is the intellect that regulates all the motions of the world, then he counts the heavens as a god, although the heavens are a part of that world which elsewhere he has entitled god.[16] And we truly can find no solutions to all these difficulties in the surviving fragments of Aristotle's dialogue *On Philosophy*. But, let us repeat, these are only Aristotle's first independent steps in creating his own system no longer dependent on Plato's.

## NOTES

[1]St. Augustine, "The Confessions" (III, 4, 7; VIII, 7, 17), *Great Books of the Western World*, 18: 14, 54, 57.

[2]*Peripatetics*: cf. pp. 79-80.

[3]Plutarch, "A Letter to Apollonius" (CXV, 27), *Moralia in 16 Volumes*, William Heinemann Ltd., London, 1971, 2: 117.

[4]*Lyceum*: cf. p. 109.

[5]"The Dialogues of Plato", *Great Books of the Western World*, 7: 135-37.

[6]Cicero, "De Oratore" (III, 35, 141), *Cicero in 28 Volumes,* Harvard University Press, Cambridge, 1977, 4: 111-13.

[7]Cicero, *Orator*, Harvard University Press, Cambridge, 1942, p. 341.

[8]Cicero, "Tusculan Disputations", *Cicero in 28 Volumes*, 18: 9-11.

[9]*The Institutio Oratoria of Quintilian* (III, 1, 13-14) *in 4 Volumes*, Harvard University Press, Cambridge, 1958, 1: 377.

[10]So-called exhortatory speeches, or *protreptici*, which had a didactic, admonitory and persuasive character, were widespread in antiquity.

[11]Plato, "The Republic", *Plato in 12 Volumes*, Harvard University Press, Cambridge, 1980, 6: 435, 441, 447-49, 449-51, 457-59.

[12]The mythical sage and musician Orpheus was considered the originator of the orphic teachings.

60

[13]"The men who were commonly regarded as sages were the follow-ing: Thales, Solon, Periander, Cleobulus, Chilon, Bias, Pittacus" (Diogenes Laertius, I, 13).

[14]Pliny's reference to this passage undoubtedly relates to Book I of the dialogue *On Philosophy,* although Valentin Rose attributed it to Aristotle's lost *Magian* on insufficient grounds.

[15]In the case of ancient philosophers, one should bear in mind the specific character of their notions of the world, i.e., the gods themselves were thought to be corporeal, woven of the finest ether.

[16]Cicero, "De Natura Deorum" (I, 13), *Cicero in 28 Volumes,* 19: 35-37.

# IV

# From the Academy to the Lyceum
# (348/7-335 BC)

## Departure from the Academy

Plato's death and the destruction of Aristotle's native town of Stagira by the troops of Philip of Macedonia deprived him of his paternal house and the second home Plato's Academy had been for him. While Plato was alive there was no element in Aristotle's spiritual development that could be detached from his mentor. But his ties with Plato's other disciples dissolved soon after his teacher's demise. Aristotle left Athens and the circle of his friends there, left the surroundings where he had spent about twenty years, and set off for Asia Minor.

Since Aristotle argued with Plato on more than one occasion during his lifetime, it could easily appear that his departure from Athens proves his break with Plato. Aristotle's character could also have provided personal motives for his departure. Some of his companions perceived his mocking tone and the implacable logic of his reasoning to be signs of demoralization. It cannot be said that the reasons for his departure were clear in antiquity. The gossip concerning Aristotle's quarrel with Plato was refuted by the intelligent and educated scholar of late antiquity Aristocles of Messana, who cited the inscription on the altar erected in Plato's honor, the wording of which was attributed to Aristotle. This inscription is fine testimony to the nature of the relations between pupil and teacher.

The first verse of the inscription speaks of a certain follower of Plato, who on his arrival in Athens instituted an altar in the name of the goddess Phyllis, sacred Friendship, and devoted it to Plato. The worship of an individual was impossible within the framework of Platonic religion, and therefore this poem deifies the ideal character of the friendship, the closeness to Plato, which joins together his faithful disciples.

A comer to the glorious land of Cecropia piously erected an altar of sacred friendship to a man whom the unworthy should not be allowed to praise; he was the only or at least the first among mortals to show manifestly with both his life and his words that a good man is at the same time a blessed one; but now nobody will ever more be able to understand this. Such are Aristotle's words concerning Plato in fragment 623.

But for all that, Aristotle's departure from Athens was a sign of inner crisis. He left Plato's school forever. He did not return to the Academy even when he subsequently came back to Athens. Plato's successor at the Academy, as we already know, was his nephew Speusippus.

Yet it was not Aristotle's critical attitude to Plato that excluded the possibility of his becoming the head of the Academy following Plato. For Speusippus had also regarded Plato's theory of the Ideas critically even during his lifetime.

One can also judge of the esteem Aristotle was held in at the Academy from the fact that he left it in the company of Xenocrates, who was reputed to be honest to the highest degree, and of all Plato's students was the most wary of any innovations. Aristotle and Xenocrates broke away from the Academy as a sign that Speusippus had not inherited Plato's spirit, only his position as head of the school. Aristotle, Xenocrates and two other Platonists, Erastus and Coriscus, settled initially in Assus on the shores of the Troad (the northwest coast of Asia Minor) for the sake of joint studies.

## Aristotle's Stay in Assus and Mytilene

Plato mentions Erastus and Coriscus in his Epistle VI, where he advises them to make peace with Hermeias, the ruler of Atarneus and Assus, the area they both came from.[1] Upon returning to their homeland after spending many years in Plato's Academy, the philosophers could not fail to enjoy great prestige. And it is not at all surprising that they were expected to do what was customary for philosophers of the time: write new laws. They also enjoyed the favor of Hermeias, who himself was keen on philosophy and was a Platonist, and who gave them the city of Assus in return for their advice on governing his state. Evidently Erastus and Coriscus successfully accomplished in Asia Minor what Plato had traveled to Sicily for. They established a milder form of constitutional rule instead of a tyranny. These reforms were effected even before Plato's death; in any case Erastus and Coriscus had received Assus from Hermeias still in his lifetime since Aristotle set off for them straight to Assus and not the neighboring city of Scepsis where they came from.

Hermeias spent a lot of time with the philosophers, and one can moreover surmise that regular lectures, not casual conversations, were held within the circle of philosophers. Aristotle became the head of the group, and Hermeias was especially well-disposed toward him. The branch of Plato's Academy at Assus became the basis for Aristotle's future school. Coriscus' son Neleus subsequently became an ardent Aristotelian, and Aristotle's closest disciple Theophrastus (360-287 BC) came from the neighboring city of Eresus on Lesbos. One understands why Coriscus' name occurs so often in Aristotle's works: Aristotle was recalling the time when his friend actually had sat in front of him during their studies in Assus. Hermeias' liking of Aristotle was so great that he married him to his adopted daughter and niece Pythias. Strabo has a sensational account of how Aristotle fled with Pythias after Hermeias was overthrown (XIII, 1, 57).[2] She bore Aristotle a daughter, also called Pythias, who was born in approximately 336 BC while Aristotle was returning to Athens from Macedonia and who was still a girl of thirteen or fourteen in the last year of Aristotle's life.

But Pythias was not Aristotle's only wife. There are reports that after her death (probably in the mid-330's) Aristotle became intimate with Herpyllis, Pythias' young maid, who bore him a son named Nicomachus in honor of Aristotle's father. Although Herpyllis was not his lawful wife, in his will Aristotle ordered his nephew Nicanor to look after her.

64

After a three-year stay in Assus Aristotle moved over to Lesbos and taught there until 343/2 BC, when he was invited to the court of King Philip of Macedonia to serve as a tutor to the king's heir Alexander. Aristotle was accompanied on this trip by Nicanor, the son of Proxenus, Aristotle's kinsman who had brought him up after his parents' death. Probably this was the same Nicanor who later played some part under Alexander the Great, was sent by him to the Olympic Games of 324 BC with the news of the amnesty of exiles and was killed in 317 BC by Cassander, the ruler of Macedonia after Alexander's death.

Soon after assuming his new duties Aristotle received news of the frightful fate that befell Hermeias who had been besieged at his residence in Atarneus by Memnon of Rhodes, a Persian general, lured out of the city by a ruse, and carried off to Susa, where he was interrogated under torture about his secret plans and conspiring with Philip, and crucified after maintaining a stubborn silence. When he was given a last wish, Hermeias requested that his friends and comrades be told that he had not betrayed philosophy or done anything unworthy of it.

One can judge of Aristotle's shock at the death of his friend and his attachment to him from the fact that he himself undertook to write the hymn to Hermeias which was chiselled on his cenotaph[3] at Delphi.

This poem, dedicated to the glorification of virtue (we shall discuss it in Chapter Six), is extremely valuable for understanding Aristotle's spiritual development. From a scientific point of view Plato's Ideas had no real existence for Aristotle, but they lived in his heart as an elevated symbol, an ideal.

However, Hermeias' death aroused quite different feelings in Athens: Demosthenes triumphantly announced that the Persian emperor had through torture forced Hermeias to confess to a plot with Philip. It must be explained that Philip was planning to declare war against the Persians, and if he came out victorious, it would allow him to legitimize his power over the Greek cities he controlled only through brute force. And Hermeias must be seen as a farsighted politician who fully realized Philip's intentions. In this connection Aristotle's appearance at Philip's court is also hardly fortuitous.

The usual account of the matter is that Philip had turned to all the famous philosophers of his time in search of tutor for Alexander. But Aristotle, pursuing philosophy with his friends in Assus and Mytilene, was not yet at the time the spiritual leader of Greece, nor was Alexander a historical figure.

The fact that Aristotle's father had once been a physician at the Macedonian court could not have played a part since that had been forty years earlier.

It is utterly out of the question that Aristotle knew nothing of Hermeias' relations with Philip. Therefore Aristotle came to Pella as the bearer of Hermeias' political ideas, in the least. His political works clearly reveal that from ethical radicalism and Platonic meditations on the ideal state Aristotle moved to the problems of actual politics. The fact that he agreed to become Alexander's tutor is a clearer evidence of his outlook than any of his compositions. This shift in Aristotle's attitude to politics occurred under the influence of Hermeias, whom Aristotle encountered when he was still under the sway of Plato's ideal model of a small city-state.

Hermeias' death increased Aristotle's antipathy to the Persians and his belief in the need for a national Greek coalition. Alexander was educated in this spirit as well.

Aristotle had no doubt that Hellas could rule the world if it were united. He did not doubt the cultural superiority of Greece over all the surrounding peoples. On the other hand, having grown up at the Macedonian court, Aristotle was unaware of the contradictions which inevitably arose in connection with any national Greek association since the political life of the Greeks was traditionally bounded by the framework of the city-state. He lacked the love of freedom characteristic of the Athenian democrats and saw nothing terrible in the unification of Greece under Macedonian dominion. For him the contradiction between patriarchal royal power and the democratic freedom of the cities could be removed only by the outstanding personality of the ruler, who would as it were embody the ideal of Greece.

This is the kind of ruler Aristotle sought in Alexander.

And it should be credited to Aristotle that although in actual fact Alexander always pursued the policies of a Macedonian king and commander, he nevertheless felt his historical mission to be tied with the fate of the Greeks, i.e., with Hellenic culture in general. In this respect he was decidedly different from Philip, who, although he recognized the necessity for Greek education, Greek technology, military science, diplomacy and rhetoric, nevertheless remained primarily a conqueror at heart. In his aesthetic and ethical education and in his pursuit of virtue, Alexander was a Greek, although this side of him was combined with a semi-barbaric, stubborn drive to become a second Achilles and take on Asia.

Of this youth Aristotle could expect that he would lead the Greeks to unity and subsequently spread their supremacy to the East through the ruins of the Persian empire.

It is true that for two years before he went to Pella, Aristotle gave lectures in Mytilene on Lesbos. The reason for his move to this place in particular may have been his closeness to Theophrastus, a native of Lesbos. The main thing here is that in his time Theophrastus had also been a pupil of Plato. Later he was Aristotle's most eminent disciple, renowned for his keen mind and power of observation. His real name was Tyrtamus, and it is Aristotle who called him Theophrastus, or Divinely Spoken. Theophrastus in turn tutored Aristotle's son Nicomachus, whom he loved very much. Theophrastus' closeness to Aristotle is attested to by the fact that in his will Aristotle appointed him his son's guardian and left him his library.

## Invitation to the Macedonian Court

Aristotle lived only two years in Mytilene, where he had moved from Assus. In 343/2 BC he was invited by Philip to tutor his thirteen-year-old son Alexander.

Quintilian, the renowned instructor in the art of oratory, correctly says that Aristotle would not have undertaken the task of tutoring Alexander if he had not thought that "the earliest instruction is best given by the most perfect teacher" (*Institutio Oratoria* I, 1, 23). In one of his speeches the rhetorician Dio Chrysostom claimed that Philip, "who is reputed to have been the cleverest of kings, engaged Aristotle as teacher and ruler for his son Alexander, believing that he himself was not competent to give instruction in the science of kingship".[4]

On the basis of Isocrates' testimony (XII, 18), some scholars conjecture that Aristotle (along with Xenocrates and Theophrastus) first went from Mytilene to Athens (also in 343/2 BC), where he spent a very short while. In that case, Philip summoned him from Athens, not Mytilene; however, the exact circumstances are not of great consequence.

Philip is usually known only as a politician who planned the conquest of Greece, Persia and other countries. But Plutarch, for one, says directly that Philip was highly interested in philosophy, art and music and did not want to entrust Alexander's schooling to ordinary teachers. He attached great importance to his son's scholarly conversations with Aristotle and even set aside a special grove near the town of Mieza for this purpose. Here Alexander and Aristotle strolled about, conducting learned conversations. (Later people would point out the stone benches on which Aristotle sat during his philosophical discourses with Alexander.)

Aelian, a by now familiar author, also reports that Philip of Macedonia was known not only to have been versed in military science and gifted with eloquence but also to have put a high value on education. Thus he put large sums at Aristotle's disposal, and thanks to him the latter was able to acquire extensive knowledge in various fields, particularly in zoology: the son of Nicomachus owed his research on animals to Philip's generosity. The king also honored Plato and Theophrastus (IV, 19).

Aristotle enjoyed great prestige at Philip's court, and when the Athenians sent an embassy to the king after the battle of Chaeronea in 338 BC, he tried to help them as best he could and get Philip to compensate for the damage and destruction he had inflicted on Greek cities.[5]

Aristotle was undoubtedly a great moral authority for Alexander, who obeyed him in many things. Wishing to call the enraged Alexander to reason and calm him down, Aristotle once wrote him that irritation and anger should be directed not at those beneath but those above, as Alexander had no equals (fragment 659). Aristotle invariably gave Alexander wise advice and therefore promoted good. Concerning Aristotle's beneficial advice we read in an ancient source that Plato was divine and pious in all other respects but ventured truly hazardous words when he said that evil among men would not cease before philosophers became kings or kings philosophers; time disproved these words. It is amazing how Aristotle, slightly altering Plato's statement, managed to make these words more truthful by saying that it was not only needful but also troublesome for a ruler to philosophize, so that it was necessary for true philosophers to give advice to a king who would be both ready to listen and quick to understand, in other words, who would fill his kingdom with good deeds and not words (fragment 647).

We would also like to note that Aristotle's enormous interest in biology and especially zoology, of which we shall speak in more detail later on, originated or in any case increased during this second stay of his in Macedonia.

## Aristotle as Tutor of Alexander

The following account in Plutarch's *Life of Alexander* shows that the king truly was well educated thanks to his talks with Aristotle: when he was waging his endless wars in the depths of Asia he did not always have books to read, and ordered the royal treasurer Harpalus "to send him some; who furnished him with Philistus's 'History', a great many of the plays of Euripides, Sophocles, and Aeschylus, and some dithyrambic odes, composed by Telestes and Philoxenus".[6]

In the same work Plutarch also writes: "Doubtless also it was to Aristotle that he owed the inclination he had, not to the theory only, but likewise to the practice of the art of medicine. For when any of his friends were sick, he would often prescribe them their course of diet, and medicines proper to their disease, as we may find in his epistles. He was naturally a great lover of all kinds of learning and reading; and Onesicritus informs us that he constantly laid

Homer's 'Iliad' according to the copy corrected by Aristotle, called the casket copy[7], with his dagger under his pillow, declaring that he esteemed it a perfect portable treasure of all military virtue and knowledge" (pp. 543-44). Onesicritus accompanied Alexander and wrote a history of his campaign in Asia which has been lost. But in view of his closeness to Alexander his information is trustworthy.

There is one more passage in Plutarch attesting to Alexander's esteem for high science, as a result of which he even had a small misunderstanding with Aristotle one day. The account which we shall quote here, is also interesting because it cites one of Alexander's letters to Aristotle: "It would appear that Alexander received from him not only his doctrines of morals and of politics, but also something of those more abstruse and profound theories which these philosophers, by the very names they gave them, professed to reserve for oral communications to the initiated, and did not allow many to become acquainted with. For when he was in Asia, and heard Aristotle had published some treatises of that kind, he wrote to him, using very plain language, on behalf of philosophy, the following letter. 'Alexander to Aristotle, greeting. You have not done well to publish your books of oral doctrine; for what is there now that we excel others in, if those things which we have been particularly instructed in be laid open to all? For my part, I assure you, I had rather excel others in the knowledge of what is excellent, than in the extent of my power and dominion. Farewell.' And Aristotle, soothing this passion for preeminence, spoke, in his excuse for himself, of these doctrines as in fact both published and not published: as indeed, to say the truth, his books on metaphysics are written in a style which makes them useless for ordinary teaching, and instructive only, in the way of memoranda, for those who have been already conversant in that sort of learning" (7, p. 543).

It is also noteworthy that Alexander had a high regard not only for Aristotle but also for those whom Aristotle respected and had told his royal pupil about. Once Alexander stopped for a few days in the city of Phaselis in Asia Minor and learned that there was a statue there of the famous rhetorician Theodectes, who had been a student of Plato, Isocrates and Aristotle himself. Plutarch gives the following account: "Finding the statue of Theodectes, who was a native of this town and was now dead, erected in the marketplace, after he had supped, having drunk pretty plentifully, he went and danced about it, and crowned it with garlands, honoring not ungracefully, in his sport, the memory of a philosopher whose conversation he had formerly enjoyed when he was Aristotle's scholar" (17, p. 548).

The education Alexander received thanks to Aristotle was quite solid and penetrated deep into the personality of the great conqueror. In any case, Aristotle wrote a book for Alexander on the way to rule and the need for a king to be good, and in reaction to it Alexander would sometimes remark that he had not ruled that day for he had not done good to anyone (fragment 646).

## Indications of Insufficient Reliability in the Accounts of Alexander's Instruction by Aristotle

If one assumes a strictly critical stance toward the testimony of the ancients, one cannot assert with great confidence that Aristotle was Alexander's sole tutor.

Since Alexander was born in 356 BC, at the time Aristotle is supposed to have been invited to the Macedonian court, i.e., in 343/2 BC, the successor to the throne was in his fourteenth year. At that age Alexander, the heir of king Philip, already had imperious habits which it would have been very difficult to eradicate. The main problem, however, is that all the information of the young prince's education by Aristotle relates to a much later period – no earlier than the first century BC.

From earlier times we know only that the cynic Onesicritus, a disciple of Diogenes of Sinope, wrote a treatise on Alexander's education along the lines of Xenophon's[8] book on the education of the Persian emperor Cyrus, in which he greatly praised the king but said nothing of Aristotle. Another historian who wrote about Macedonia, Marsyas of Pella, came from a distinguished Macedonian family and, according to him, studied with Alexander; but he does not mention Aristotle either. A third early Greek historian, Alexinus, a younger contemporary of Aristotle,

71

although mentioning the philosopher, reports at the same time that already as a youth Alexander spoke of him with scorn. The sense of himself being not only a Greek but a citizen of the world which was attributed to Alexander was not at all typical of Aristotle. It relates rather to the views of the cynic philosophers, particularly the above-mentioned Onesicritus, who was one of Alexander's favorites. Under the circumstances the question arises as to whether Alexander really was a disciple of Aristotle and whether he was not at the same time the pupil of one of the cynics, especially when one considers his respect for Diogenes of Sinope.

If one turns from the earlier to later historians, Plutarch before referring to Aristotle mentions two other tutors of Alexander — Leonidas, a relative of Alexander's mother Olympias, and Lysimachus the Acarnanian (5, p. 542) — and lists Aristotle only in third place (17, p. 548). Xenocrates, who was even entrusted with writing a manual on royal power, might have had no less importance for Alexander. If such is the case, could Aristotle and Xenocrates have been rivals at the Macedonian court, since they were both students of Plato, left the Academy at the same time and both went to the north?

Quintilian directly states that Alexander's main teacher was neither Aristotle nor Xenocrates but the Leonidas mentioned by Plutarch, whom Quintilian holds responsible for many faults in Alexander's character which clung to him even in his maturer years (I, 1, 9).

Aristotle's Arab biographers, who highly esteemed Aristotle, either confine themselves simply to mentioning that among Aristotle's pupils was Alexander, or say nothing at all about Aristotle's mentorship. Not Aristotle but Onesicritus accompanied Alexander on his campaigns to Asia. And the centuries-old tradition of the stoic philosophers with their concern for the education of the ideal person also says nothing of Alexander's schooling under Aristotle. Clement of Alexandria blames Alexander's irascibility, cruelty and other faults on his education under Leonidas, not mentioning Aristotle.

Probably a certain literary tradition arose in late antiquity of boundlessly praising Alexander and his virtues (while forgetting his monstrous crimes) and boundlessly lauding Aristotle as his ideal pedagogue and preceptor. Aulus Gellius even cites a whole letter supposedly written by Philip to Aristotle after Alexander's birth in 356 BC where he expresses the wish to have Aristotle be the future tutor of his son.[9] But if one correlates the chronological data, it turns out that at that time Aristotle himself was still studying under Plato and was only twenty-eight years old. Could Philip really have known of Aristotle's existence already then and realized that he would become a great thinker and pedagogue? Without doubt a letter of this type from Philip was only a literary fiction composed for the purposes of the tradition then developing of trying at all costs to join together the greatest conqueror and the greatest thinker.

All these facts which cast doubt on Aristotle's commanding role as mentor in Alexander's life and fate cannot be immediately and categorically tossed aside in favor of other ancient accounts of Aristotle and Alexander's close relations. Such exaggerations, sometimes frankly improbable, were rife in late antiquity. Just consider, for instance, the image favored by ancient writers, of Alexander surrounded by all kinds of miracles and fantastic events which supposedly accompanied him everywhere! But even apart from the supernatural, many writers and readers of the time were extremely fond of the idea of this touching friendship between a pupil and teacher, where the pupil had conquered half the world and the teacher was a celebrated thinker. Upon analyzing the numerous and often contradictory facts, we are obliged to proceed with extreme caution, which leads us to take a sort of middle stand on the issue of Alexander's instruction by Aristotle. One cannot entirely dismiss Aristotle's influence on Alexander. Such major ancient writers as Dionysius of Halicarnassus, Eratosthenes, Quintilian, Plutarch, Dio Chrysostom and especially Diogenes Laertius insist on Aristotle's tutelage of Alexander and influence on him. Yet one should also not raise the relationship between two great men to the status of some absolute ideal. Finally, one must reckon with the possible untrustworthiness of many accounts current since antiquity, their frequent obscurity and incomplete demonstrability.

# NOTES

[1]Plato, *Epistles,* Harvard University Press, Cambridge; William Heinemann Ltd., London, 1981, 9: p. 457.

[2]*The Geography of Strabo in 8 Volumes,* Harvard University Press, Cambridge, 1950, 6: 115-17.

[3]*Cenotaph* (literally, "empty tomb"): a monument erected to a person whose remains lie elsewhere.

[4]*The Forty-Ninth Discourse on Kingship* (4), William Heinemann Ltd., London, 1946, 6: 297.

[5]In fact Diogenes Laertius reports that Aristotle was himself part of this delegation, to which he assigns an earlier date, 339 BC (IV, 8, 9).

[6]Plutarch, "The Lives of the Noble Grecians and Romans. — Alexander" (8), *Great Books of the Western World*, 14: 544.

[7]This valuable casket was seized from Darius, and Alexander kept in it the things that were most precious to him.

[8]*Xenophon*: famous ancient Greek historian and philosopher of the fifth and fourth centuries BC, a follower of Socrates and contemporary of Plato.

[9]Aulus Gellius, *The Attic Nights in 3 Volumes* (IX, 3), William Heinemann Ltd., London, 1968, 2: 159-61.

# Lyceum (335-322 BC)

## The Founding of the Lyceum

Aristotle did not spend a great many years at Philip's court. Alexander's military and political enterprises prospered and he could not devote much time to studying. Already as a seventeen-year-old youth he was the ruler in the Macedonian capital of Pella while Philip was away. Aristotle often did not have the time to instruct and train his royal pupil.

But the most important circumstance was Philip's assassination in the summer of 336 BC by one of his bodyguards, Pausanias; Alexander became the head of state and now had other things on his mind than studying.

Remaining on the best of terms with Alexander, Aristotle decided to leave Pella that same year and, feeling himself a mature philosopher (he was about fifty at the time), he resolved to settle in the city he had once left, Athens itself. Thus he spent about eight years at the Macedonian court.[1]

However, if one is to observe chronological order, the information provided by our main source (Diogenes Laertius, who refers himself to Apollodorus — V, 9-10) concerning Aristotle's return to Athens in the second year of the third Olympiad admits of different interpretations: it could have been either in the fall of 335 BC or in the spring of 334 BC. A scholar has even suggested that Aristotle did not head straight for Athens but stopped in Stagira on the way. But this hypothesis is very debatable, and if it really was so, Aristotle's stay in Stagira could have lasted only a few months.

In Athens Aristotle's first task was, of course, to found his own school, for by that time his philosophical divergence from Platonism had become quite perceptible. There was no longer any place for him within the Academy.

Speusippus, Plato's first successor, did not remain at the head of the Academy for long. Hot-tempered, impulsive and somewhat gloomy, he was also seriously ill. The Academy needed the firm hand of Xenocrates, who had become a most prominent figure by that time. Diogenes Laertius reports of Speusippus: "When he was already crippled by paralysis, he sent a message to Xenocrates entreating him to come and take over the charge of the school" (IV, 3). Judging from the letters which Speusippus is reputed to have sent Xenocrates, things were not going well at the Academy. In one, the ailing Speusippus told Xenocrates that he had thought it necessary to write him of his physical condition since he believed that Xenocrates would get the whole school back into shape if he returned to the Academy; since Plato had valued him highly and declared as much at the end of his life, Speusippus now advised him to show his gratitude to Plato, a deed he considered fine and just, by coming to the Academy and taking the school into his hands: such firmness and faithfulness could justifiably be called true wisdom (Letter 30). In another, he urgently summoned Xenocrates, saying that for a long time he had wanted him to come, but that it would be a good thing if he came even now; for he would be put in charge of Speusippus' affairs and take proper care of the business of the school (Letter 31).

Xenocrates did not tarry. Returning to Athens after a ten-year absence, he became the head of the Academy after Speusippus' death and ran it for full twenty-five years (339-314 BC).

Aristotle came to Athens in 335 BC, when the friend of his youth Xenocrates, with whom he had once left the Academy, had been directing the school for four years already. Incidentally, Diogenes Laertius informs us that Aristotle purchased the works of Speusippus after his death for three talents (IV, 5).[2]

One can say for sure that if Aristotle did not stay at the Academy it was only on account of profound differences with its new head.

One cannot speak of philosophical closeness between Aristotle and Xenocrates in the absolute sense of the word. The fact is that Xenocrates had considerably reworked Platonism and in the end come up with a number of theories which went far beyond the limits of Plato's philosophy; Aristotle had done the same with Plato's legacy, only in a different direction. There were probably also non-philosophical reasons for Aristotle's differences with Xenocrates, and these may have been rooted in the latter's character.

Xenocrates was always "dignified and grave of demeanor" (Diogenes Laertius, IV, 6-10) and was distinguished for his truthfulness, integrity and self-possession. Without being haughty, Xenocrates nevertheless was hard to approach, quite incorruptible and really too dignified. Even the then-renowned and irresistible courtesan Phryne was unable to tempt him. Xenocrates was famous for his enormous self-control and could even endure cauterization for medicinal purposes.

Xenocrates conducted himself independently. Once Alexander sent him a large sum of money as a gift, but he kept only 3000 Attic drachmae and sent back the rest, saying the king was more in need of this money for the wants of his people. From Antipater, Alexander's military commander, he did not accept any presents at all, and once did not even answer his greeting immediately, but only after finishing his philosophical discourse. Xenocrates' incorruptibility and uprightness were such that the Athenians allowed him to bear witness in court without taking an oath, although this was forbidden by law. And when he was sent to Philip with other envoys, he behaved independently and did not flatter the king like the others. In this connection Philip later said that he had learned who in Greece was mercenary and who was not to be bought. When Xenocrates was sent to request the freeing of the Athenian prisoners taken in the Lamian war (322 BC), he once again treated Antipater in a most familiar and original manner. He did not bother spending any time preparing a speech, but confined himself to reciting the famous verses from Homer's *Odyssey* recounting the freeing of Odysseus' companions from bondage to the enchantress Circe (X, 383-385).[3] To the gibes of a certain Bion, Xenocrates responded rather arrogantly that he would make no retort as it was unworthy of tragedy to criticize comedy. For failing to pay some taxes he was almost sold into slavery. Significant in itself is the fact that when he would leave the Academy to go into town litter-bearers would rush to clear the way for him.

It is only natural that Aristotle did not feel like staying at the Academy under Xenocrates. One can guess at the rivalry between these two philosophers in Alexander's eyes from the following fact. When he left Pella in 335 BC Aristotle had recommended his kinsman Callisthenes as an advisor, secretary and historian to Alexander. Subsequently Callisthenes proved to have been part of a conspiracy against Alexander in 327 BC and was executed on his order. Afterwards, to humiliate Aristotle on Callisthenes' account, the king began to give rich gifts to Xenocrates. Such a state of affairs could hardly have improved relations between the two philosophers.

Aristotle established his new school in Athens near the temple of Apollo Lycius, situated in the northeast section of the city and giving the locality the name of Lyceum. Both Apollo's shrine and the Lyceum had existed from time immemorial in Athens.[4]

Xenophon mentions that the Lyceum was a place for horseback riding.[5] A gymnasium was also located there.[6] It had been built by Lycurgus, an opponent of the tyrant Pisistratus, to whom the building of the gymnasium was also attributed; Pericles as well figures as the founder of the gymnasium. Thus the Lyceum had existed for a hundred or even two hundred years before Aristotle. In any case, the sophists had pursued their studies here and their school had arisen in the fifth century BC and aimed at studying man with all his subjective moods, in contrast to more ancient philosophers, who primarily studied nature and the cosmos. It is in this ancient Lyceum that Aristotle began to teach after his return to Athens.

The Lyceum was later destroyed twice: by Philip in about 200 BC and by the Roman general Sulla around 87 BC during the siege of Athens, when Plato's Academy also suffered.

## The Lyceum, Peripat, and the Academy

From days of old *peripat*[7] was the name given in Athens to municipal gardens meant for strolling. The founders of philosophical schools often used these gardens to assemble the public, give lectures, and hold philosophical discussions in general. This happened all the more naturally since the various *peripats* usually adjoined gymnasia, i.e., places originally intended for gymnastic exercises but subsequently for all kinds of schooling. The *peripats* were widely used by philosophers and scholars for instructional purposes, and later the term came to mean a school generally or philosophical school: it became synonymous with the words *school* or *diatribe* (the latter originally meaning conversation, argument, interrelation).

The most famous gymnasia with an adjoining *peripat* were the Academy, the Lyceum and the Cynosarges (the school of the cynic philosophers). The site called the Academy was acquired by Plato and therefore belonged only to him. As for the Lyceum, Aristotle as a native of the provinces, or in the language of the time a *metek* (migrant), did not have the right to acquire landed property in Athens. The *peripat* which Aristotle used for teaching was bought after his death by his student Theophrastus. From that time the *peripat* of the Lyceum gave its name to Aristotle's school.

A remark is in order here. The word *Peripatetic,* referring to a representative of Aristotle's school, is hardly connected directly with the idea of teaching while strolling. For it was the custom of other philosophers as well, and not only Aristotle, to teach while walking. Plato, for instance, also gave his lectures and conversed while walking; Epicurus speaks directly of "the Peripatetic Plato" (fragment 171).[8] From Cicero's writings we can conclude that Plato's disciples were initially also called Peripatetics[9] and were at first termed "the Peripatetics of the Academy" to distinguish them from "the Peripatetics of the Lyceum", Aristotle's disciples, and only later did Plato's followers come to be called simply Academicians, and Aristotle's, or the Aristotelians, Peripatetics. The Lyceum and the Academy differed fundamentally in their philosophical teachings, but even in their structure and customs there were many differences which emphasized the rivalry between these two schools. In the Lyceum, linked from ancient times with the name of the god Apollo, there was a temple to Apollo Lycius. In the Academy, there was a sanctuary of Athena, the muses and the hero Akademos, and an altar to Prometheus. The Lyceum had an ancient gymnasium; the Academy also had one, which was even older. At his Academy Plato conducted scholarly conversations while strolling around the *peripat*. The Lyceum had its own *peripat*, where Aristotle, following ancient tradition, also conversed with his pupils. The Academy was located to the northwest of Athens, six stadia (a little over a mile) away, beyond the Dipylon Gate, while the Lyceum lay to the east of Athens near the city wall by the Gate of Diochares, where there were springs with wonderful drinking water. And quite close to the Lyceum another of Plato's students, the cynic Antisthenes, founded his own school, the Cynosarges, also with a gymnasium and *peripat*.

The road to the Academy passed through Ceramicus, where funerary stelae were erected to famous Athenians. The Lyceum was situated near the road to Marathon, famous from the Greco-Persian war. From the Academy one could see the hills and olive groves of Colonus, the birthplace of Sophocles. From the gardens of the Lyceum there was a view of Mount Lycabettus, linked with the god Apollo. The site of the Academy was Plato's private property. But the Lyceum, founded in 335 BC, was not legally Aristotle's right up to his death.

From the moment it was formed Plato's Academy can be called a school. One can refer to the Lyceum as a philosophical school in the proper sense of the word not starting in 335 BC, if one is to be precise, but only from 322 BC when Aristotle died and the head of the school, his closest disciple Theophrastus, a lawful Athenian citizen, finally became the owner of the Lyceum. Plato spent all his life in Athens, returning from his trips to Sicily to his own home, his Academy. Aristotle did not live all that long in Athens, was always considered an alien, and his life was not very serene.

Aristotle worked indefatigably in his Lyceum. In the morning he gave lectures for a select group of listeners on the most difficult points of his philosophy. But he also

80

gave afternoon classes in a large auditorium for less-prepared students. These afternoon and evening courses were devoted to relatively accessible issues, in particular to questions of rhetoric. Here Aristotle even had his own distinctive school in the art of oratory, a fact which in itself portrays him not only as an absorbed philosopher, retired from the world, but also as a person concerned with the general problems of life.

The *Rhetoric* that has come down to us attests to his enormous interest in various everyday situations and his amazing ability to get to the bottom of them. One can conclude that the philosopher's "evening-class students", if one may so call them, were supremely lucky people, since they could learn to analyze complex life situations and to speak about them in an enlightened, competent, elegant manner.

Aristotle established one other noteworthy custom at the Lyceum. He regularly dined with his friends, conducting scholarly discussions with them at the same time. And like everything else where Aristotle was concerned, these dinners had a systematic character, to the point that every ten days a new chairman was elected for them, and Aristotle himself even wrote a special memorandum for these scholarly dinners entitled "Laws of the Mess Table". Moreover, from the biographical information we have about Aristotle we can infer that such "laws" and attendants to their observance, whom we would now call monitors, were instituted by Aristotle for the whole school in general, or perhaps only for the conversation hours.

The Lyceum undoubtedly had to dispose of a library of no small dimensions, as is apparent from Aristotle's works, those whose authenticity is unquestionable. They are packed with precise references to various authors and quotations from them which would be unthinkable without a large library. Without a doubt, too, Aristotle had to make use of the help of his patrons Philip and Alexander to sustain the existence and development of all these studies and scholarly and scientific endeavors at the Lyceum. According to the writer Athenaeus, Alexander gave Aristotle no less than eight hundred talents to further his zoological research (*The Deipnosophists* IX, 398e). But perhaps no less important is the communication by Pliny

81

the Elder that Alexander put at Aristotle's disposal, also to aid in his zoological investigations, "all those who made their living by hunting, fowling, and fishing and those who were in charge of warrens, herds, apiaries, fishponds and aviaries".[10]

This report sounds too exaggerated, and some scholars have questioned its reliability. But in any event one cannot deny that Aristotle's Lyceum received substantial assistance from highly-placed patrons to pursue its extensive research and teaching activities.

There were peculiarities in the very organization of the Lyceum which indicated the entirely new features characteristic of Aristotle's philosophy and foreign to Plato's. The practical direction of the Lyceum and the multitude of concrete investigations undertaken by Aristotle and his students showed that philosophy within Aristotle's school was understood and taught differently from the way it had been by Plato. The difference must not of course be exaggerated and taken to an extreme. But with it in mind, it is proper to show how the transition occurred from one type of philosophizing at Plato's Academy to another kind at Aristotle's Lyceum.

### Aristotle, and Plato's Academy

Plato and Aristotle are two different philosophers who are generally thought to be utterly incompatible. It is as though Aristotelianism had been chopped off with an axe from Platonism and had only become true Aristotelianism in this anti-Platonic condition. Views of this sort are not only customary among the public at large but have found their way into many textbooks and shown up in a number of scholarly studies. Such sharp contrasting of different epochs or individual figures within one era has been rejected nowadays, even if one must still take into account the opposition and antagonism between cultural phenomena originating from the same foundations.

Yes, as we shall see below, Aristotle really is contrary to Plato. But Aristotle's philosophy, thus opposed to Plato's, could in no way have emerged instantaneously; Aristotelianism arose only gradually on the soil of Platonism, both through the appearance of new features alien to Plato's philosophy and through the retention and even further development of elements of Platonism. As we read deeper into Aristotle's works, we keep coming across echoes of Plato's thoughts, which stayed with Aristotle to the day he died.

As we saw earlier, Aristotle appeared at the Academy in 367/6 BC. Is it of no significance that the Academy had arisen in approximately 387 BC, at least twenty years before Aristotle entered it and met the sixty-year-old Plato, already wise with experience? Can it be that the brilliant Plato had not gone through a certain course of development up to that time and that the young Aristotle, who was also to be a philosopher of genius, did not find the Academy at a definite historical period of its existence, at a definite stage in its spiritual development?

By then Plato had already produced his main philosophico-mythological works. He had already written the *Phaedrus*, *Symposium*, *Phaedo* and *Republic*. Moreover, a shift had become evident in Plato's approach from mythophilosophic and artistic constructions toward much more theoretical, often abstractly dialectic and systematically complete structures. The dialogue *Theaetetus*, written around 369 BC, or about two years before Aristotle's enrollment in the Academy, can be seen as such a turning-point.

Of course admiration of Plato's earlier works never faded at the Academy nor, one can say, in all of ancient philosophy up to the last centuries of its existence. Nonetheless at the Academy Aristotle not only encountered philosophico-religious and mytho-artistic problems but also the actual teachings on the dialectic of concepts. For already in the *Theaetetus* purely gnoseological issues (i.e., relating to the theory of knowledge) were raised and grappled with, tasks essential to establishing the logic of cognition.

*Theaetetus* is grounded on the assertion of the continuous fluctuation of all that exists; and the question is posed: can the philosopher remain within the limits of uninterrupted and chaotic fluidity? It appears that human cognition is possible only provided that the stable Ideas exist, through the help of which one can comprehend fluid reality and trace in it some kind of logical order. In this connection anyone must recognize that the basic problem in the *Theaetetus* is a purely gnoseological (epistemological) one or, generally speaking, a systemic and logical one. The *Theaetetus* was followed by Plato's *Parmenides, Sophist, Politicus (Statesman)* and *Philebus,* all dialogues in which the constructive and logical element predominates. It is at this stage in the development of the Academy that Aristotle entered it.

But if the history of Aristotle's spiritual development and activity at the Lyceum is of importance to us, we must dwell on a very essential fact in his biography: around 367 BC Aristotle met a remarkable person at the Academy, Eudoxus of Cnidos.

## Eudoxus of Cnidos

Eudoxus was born around 408 BC (according to other accounts, in 391 BC) on the island of Cnidos off the coast of Asia Minor, in the city of Cnidos, known as one of the main centers of worship of the goddess Aphrodite, in whose honor the Greek sculptor Praxiteles chiselled his famous statue. The heyday of Eudoxus' philosophical career was in 368-365 BC, during his second stay in Athens. He died around 355 BC at the age of fifty-three.

Eudoxus came to Athens for the first time at the age of twenty-three, i.e., around 385 BC. It is possible that he began to attend Plato's lectures already then. In addition, the sources say that he studied under the Pythagorean Archytas, who instructed him in astronomy and geometry; and he also studied medicine under famous doctors of the time. There are also reports that he travelled to Egypt in approximately 381/0 BC. In Strabo's version (XVII, 1, 29), he even went to Egypt with Plato and spent a whole of thirteen years there, prevailing with difficulty upon the Egyptian priests to impart some of their doctrines. Then Eudoxus spent a few years in Cyzicus and Pergamum in Asia Minor, and returned to Athens, this time with a whole school of disciples, so that Diogenes Laertius even refers to a certain rivalry between Eudoxus and Plato (VIII, 87). That was hardly the case since there is scholarly evidence of Eudoxus' Platonism. In any event, during Plato's second trip to Sicily (367-365 BC), Eudoxus served for him as head of the Academy. This is only natural as the two of them were old friends from the time of their joint journey to Egypt.

Some time afterwards (approximately six or seven years later), Eudoxus returned to Cnidos, where he was invested with full legislative powers. He had had his own philosophical school before he came to the Academy, and he did not stay at the Academy to the end of his life, but returned to his native town a few years before his death. Thus he was not a Platonic Academician in the proper sense of the word, but merely spent his prime years at the Academy.

Perhaps Eudoxus of Cnidos should not be considered a Platonist in the full sense of the term, although he even visited Plato in Sicily around 361 BC. Aristotle speaks of Eudoxus with great affection and in so doing reveals a line of thinking characteristic not of Plato but of Eudoxus and Aristotle himself.

*Eudoxus as the Transition Between Plato and Aristotle.* A passage from the *Nicomachean Ethics* where Eudoxus' teaching on pleasure is sympathetically examined shows Aristotle's closeness to Eudoxus. Neither Plato nor Aristotle holds pleasure to be the highest good. Nevertheless it enters into this greatest good with a certain modification. The text which we cite below attests to Aristotle's great affinity with Eudoxus: "Eudoxus thought pleasure was the good because he saw all things, both rational and irrational, aiming at it, and because in all things that which is the object of choice is what is excellent and that which is most the object of choice the greatest good; thus the fact that all things moved toward the same object indicated that this was for all things the chief good (for each thing, he argued, finds its own good, as it finds its own nourishment); and that which is good for all things and at which all aim was *the* good. His arguments were credited more because of the excellence of his character than for their own sake; he was thought to be remarkably self-controlled, and therefore it was thought that he was not saying what he did say as a friend of pleasure, but that the facts really were so. He believed that the same conclusion followed no

85

less plainly from a study of the contrary of pleasure; pain was in itself an object of aversion to all things, and therefore its contrary must be similarly an object of choice. And again that is most an object of choice which we choose not because or for the sake of something else, and pleasure is admittedly of this nature; for no one asks to what end he is pleased, thus implying that pleasure is in itself an object of choice" (X, 2).

Aristotle's closeness to Eudoxus on some issues was balanced by divergences on some others, but these differences did not come in the way of the two philosophers' personal friendship.

Eudoxus' closeness to Plato and Aristotle is evidenced by the fact that he considered the circle or sphere and circular motion to be most perfect, and on the basis of various mathematical computations proved the sphericality of the cosmos as a whole, and of all the then-known luminaries and planets as well.

*Eudoxus' Theory of a Spherical Cosmos in Relation to Other Ancient Greek Sense-Based Theories of the Cosmos*. There is no need to be surprised that the Platonist Eudoxus, like Plato himself, imagined the cosmos and the main motions of the heavenly bodies to be spherical. Let us not forget that the Greek ethos in general was primarily based on visual perception and that the whole cosmos was conceived visually most often as a sphere. For Thales the cosmos was a round plate floating on the water, with the bottom of this plate turned upward, not downward. Anaximander imagined the cosmos as a cylinder, but this cylinder was surrounded by circles of fire. Thus in Anaximander's words we also find a globe-shaped heaven, consisting of some sort of fiery "rings", and the heavenly bodies presented as openings in these rings, thanks to which the fire within the globe becomes visible. One encounters no less than five attempts by Plato to picture the shape of the cosmos. And one of them also presents a spherical sky; but the axis of the universe is depicted as a cosmic spindle around which the heavenly spheres revolve. For Empedocles the cosmos would now appear, now perish in flame, and there was no end to this eternal return. Democritus also believed each individual cosmos to be finite, and for him ours had appeared out of a vortex, a violent and chaotic motion of atoms. But according to Democritus there is an infinite number of such universes, so that in the final analysis the world is unending. After all this, is it so surprising that the universe should be sphere-shaped for Eudoxus too, and that this sphericality of the cosmos is characteristic of both Plato and Aristotle as well?

*Mutual Influence of Plato and Eudoxus.* However, it is probably Eudoxus who introduced to the Academy a very important idea, which we shall discuss below and which was based on the method of so-called **exhaustion**, which stressed the idea of infinity within the bounds of the general spherical conceptions of the cosmos.

Aristotle also points to Eudoxus' differences with Plato. Specifically, in criticizing the isolated world of Platonic Ideas in his *Metaphysics* (I, 9), he asserts that the ideas of things explain nothing in the things themselves, even if we accept the teaching of Anaxagoras and Eudoxus that the idea of the thing (note that Anaxagoras himself does not use the term "idea") relates to the thing itself as whiteness relates to a white object. In other words, Eudoxus in contrast to Plato was inclined to view all the ideal as a variety of the material, hence his whole theory of spheres was not pure idealism but merely a refined materialism.

Probably Eudoxus really did represent some kind of transition between Plato and Aristotle, since Aristotle himself did not at all deny the independent existence of the ideas, but attributed to them existence inside individual things. One cannot but consider such an intermediate link between Plato and Aristotle a remarkable phenomenon in the history of philosophy.

It must be kept in mind that Eudoxus was also renowned as an expert in many empirical sciences. He was primarily a mathematician and an astronomer, but the sources also speak of his works in the fields of medicine, geography and ethnography. All sciences of this kind were developing successfully in various parts of Greece, but although sometimes they were fused in the work of one particular thinker, they had never before been summarized in a few clear principles.

As Plato's students, Eudoxus and then Aristotle became the first thinkers to join empirical and theoretical knowledge. It can in no way be denied that Plato exerted enormous influence on these two philosophers, even though the most flourishing of all the sciences at the Academy itself were mathematics and astronomy, the two farthest removed from precise and detailed empirical investigation. Nevertheless the Academy, as we have just stated, had arrived at the elucidation of the logical unity of human knowledge. All that was left was to apply this theory concerning fundamental principles to empirical research, and it fell to the lot of Eudoxus and Aristotle to do so. But if we keep strictly to the facts of the history of philosophy and philology, it must be remembered that it was Socrates, always aiming for generalizations that could not be reduced to individual observed facts, who had already long since elaborated the principle of the unity of concepts. Plato himself had begun his career precisely by examining these generalized concepts.

### Eudoxus' Method of Exhaustion

**Eudoxus' method of "exhaustion" is a way of merging Plato's Ideas of things with the things themselves, where the Idea of the thing does not remain in isolated existence but finds expression in the things as their principle and method, as the law of their actual coming-to-be.** But to the Socratic theory of universalized meaning Plato contributed an extremely important principle, which found its most pronounced expression in Eudoxus' work, namely the so-called principle of exhaustion. This principle will become clear to us after an examination of the main difference between Plato and Aristotle concerning the correlation of Idea and matter.

Despite his great intellectual bias in favor of the existence of these generalizations, or as he put it, these *eidos* or Ideas, Plato was always put off by a complete dualism of Ideas and matter. Of course in studying these ideas in themselves, without the things to give meaning to which they were actually first formulated, it is very easy to cut oneself off from the study of the things themselves. Furthermore such separation of the two is sometimes necessary for a precise and attentive study of them independently of each other. In the *Parmenides*, for instance, Plato outlines a remarkable abstract dialectic of the Ideas in which there is not a word about any sensual things. But this rupture is not a matter of principle for Plato. It is maintained only for convenience and clarity of his dialectical analysis, as every one of his dialogues, and especially the *Parmenides,* shows us. *Parmenides* in particular contains a detailed discussion of the inadmissibility of the isolated, independent existence of Ideas and things, and in no uncertain terms recognizes not only the separate existence of Ideas and things, but also their most intimate interaction.[11] Such reasoning on Plato's part would hardly have been possible without the intervention of Eudoxus, who had an enormous significance for Aristotle as well.

In the end all these philosophers agree that the idea of the thing, whether it exists outside the thing or inside it, is in any event necessary for the cognition of each individual thing. Plato only foregrounds the generalized existence of the Ideas, without however denying the Ideas of individual things; whereas Aristotle gives pride of place precisely to these particular Ideas, without at the same time denying the general existence of the world of Ideas as a whole. Later we shall see that Aristotle develops even further the Platonic doctrine of the general existence of a world of Ideas, calling it the cosmic Mind and Prime Mover. And it was in order to explain how one could pass from the conception of the Idea of a thing to the existence of the thing itself and, conversely, from a concrete thing to the Idea itself of the thing that Eudoxus came up with his **exhaustive method**.

As we know, Eudoxus was primarily a student of empirical knowledge, albeit generalized. Empirical knowledge, based on direct observation of phenomena, attests to the continuous mutability and fluctuation of the material world, so uninterrupted that it is impossible even to record each individual thing and its specific character. Heraclitus, Empedocles and Anaxagoras already well understood this. What are we to do now in our quest for exact empirical knowledge if everything is continuously and uninterruptedly in flux? Plato put forward the concept of the Ideas, those supports in the midst of continuous flux which are its landmarks as it were and allow one to get to identify and record it. But for this to be true the idea itself must be suf-

89

ficiently flexible and fluid, otherwise it will only comprehend separate discontinuous markers in the flow, not fluctuation as such. The idea of the thing had to be understood not only as firm and stable, but as a principle of instability and variability as well. The idea itself of the thing is fixed. But to ground a theory of knowledge it was necessary that this steady Idea serve as the foundation for all the instability and fluidity of the corresponding thing. It was here that Eudoxus' method came in handy.

In studying Plato we find that each Idea can and must undergo endless division, as is also true of each thing. This can full well be called a classical theory of least values. In the Modern Era the term "infinitely small" has come to refer to what **can become** smaller than any given quantity. The infinitely small is not some fixed magnitude which would not allow of any further division. Division cannot stop anywhere and ever, does not lead to some stationary, albeit very small, substance; rather the infinitely small is the **process** of infinite division, insofar as between two points on a line, however close they may be to each other, one can always imagine a third point.

Thus in its very essence the idea of the thing is nothing other than the **principle** of endless division or, generally speaking, endless transformation of the thing itself. It also needs saying that the living idea of things must be the **principle of their coming into being** and the real **law** of their origin. If we know what the thing itself is, i.e., what constitutes its essence and idea, then we will be able to judge both how this thing changes and what it is at a given moment of its existence. But if we do not know what the idea of the thing is, then we do not know either what the thing itself is or what it is at a given moment of its existence. This is why ideas are needed to cognize things in flux, and things in flux, to cognize the ideas.

The universal does not exist without the particular, nor the particular without the universal.

The universal is the law for the appearance of the particular, and the particular is the natural result of the functioning of the universal.

*Aristotle and Eudoxus*. Thus one can say that Eudoxus enlivened the Platonic Idea by understanding it as the

90

principle of the empirical existence of things. It must immediately be noted that Aristotle also established and elaborated the **principle of fragmentation of substances**, or exhaustive method, as being a **law** necessary for the cognition of empirical reality in general.

This principle lay at the basis of all of Aristotle's later philosophy.

And so, as we see, Eudoxus played a very important role in Aristotle's intellectual development, and consequently in the advance of the philosophical theory which was recognized at the Lyceum.

### The General Attitude Toward Philosophy at the Lyceum

We shall not be mistaken if we say that Aristotle's whole philosophy—which took shape at the Lyceum—is nothing but a **eulogy to reason** and the reasonable life. In confirmation we could cite a host of diverse passages from Aristotle, but we shall content ourselves here with referring the reader to the *Nicomachean Ethics* (I, 3), *Eudemian Ethics* (I, 5)[12] and the *Magna Moralia* (I, 4; II, 6).[13]

*Careful Historicism and Systematized Scholarly Philosophical Research*. We are struck by Aristotle's meticulousness in going over earlier philosophical material before coming out with some more or less conclusive formulation of his own regarding the problem under study. The very beginning of the *Metaphysics* contains abundant material from previous philosophers along with a critical analysis, and only then does Aristotle make up his mind to start speaking of his "first philosophy". He mentions such philosophers as Thales, Anaximenes, Heraclitus, Anaxagoras, Xenophon, Empedocles, Parmenides, Melissus, Diogenes of Apollonia, the Pythagoreans, Leucippus, Democritus, Cratylus, Socrates, Plato and so on. In the *Nicomachean Ethics* (X, 9), he finds it necessary first to examine the opinions of his predecessors on the organization of the state and only then to speak of it himself. In the *Rhetoric* we read that "what is long established seems akin to what exists by nature ... what appears to have been always what it is is regarded as real" (II, 9). In other words it is natural for the philosopher to study the facts of the past; and the community of opinion of his precursors, or as Aristotle here expresses it, "what appears to have been always what it is", confirms and strengthens him on his way toward the truth. That is why it is a prerequisite to study each question in its historical development. In the *Topics*, for instance, he speaks at length of the need to study not only the subjects of one's investigation, but their opposites as well (I, 14). This means that one should examine the opinions of former philosophers who do not concur with each other, i.e., truth is reached no longer through shared opinions but by overcoming differences.

Thus at the Lyceum Aristotle taught philosophy, first, strictly historically and, second, strictly systematically. Both methods of understanding philosophy are necessary because "the same ideas, one must believe, recur in men's minds not once or twice but again and again" (*On the Heavens* I, 3).

In the third place it is clear that Aristotle also requires a very calm and methodically self-possessed attitude to philosophy. In fragment 27 of a biography of Aristotle by an unknown author we read that he had a very moderate disposition; and the biographer goes on to cite a passage from Aristotle's *Categories* to the effect that one must not express one's opinion precipitously but only after considering it many times, and that perplexity is not always injurious. In his work *On the Good* Aristotle writes that not only when experiencing happiness must you remember that you are only a mere mortal, but also when constructing proofs which do not always immediately assume a flawless form (fragment 22).

### Practical Activity and Contemplation

**It is inherent not only in an unreasoning being to come into being, but in reason itself, in which case, however, this coming into being has a quite specific and moreover blissful quality in view of its all-embracing universality.** It is also interesting to find that in his attitude to philosophy Aristotle (and hence all his school) was in a remarkable way able to conjoin practical empirical research with the tranquil, unperturbed and blissful state of pure reason.

Aristotle would say that just as a horse is born for running, an ox for ploughing and a dog for hunting out, man is born for two things, intellectual comprehension and action, like some mortal god (fragment 61).

On the one hand, practical life is best of all, according to Aristotle. "And it is equally a mistake to place inactivity above action, for happiness is activity, and the actions of the just and wise are the realization of much that is noble" (*Politics* VII, 3). Furthermore, "the answer to the question we are asking is plain also from the definition of happiness; for it has been said to be a virtuous activity of soul, of a certain kind" (*Nicomachean Ethics* I, 9). On the other hand, reason is portrayed by Aristotle as that which is most universal and most essential, and practical and blissful. The following passage from the *Nicomachean Ethics* (VI, 6) makes a particularly deep impression on the reader: "Scientific knowledge is judgment about things that are universal and necessary, and the conclusions of demonstration, and all scientific knowledge, follow from first principles (for scientific knowledge involves apprehension of a rational ground). This being so, the first principle from which what is scientifically known follows cannot be an object of scientific knowledge, or art, or of practical wisdom; for that which can be scientifically known can be demonstrated, and art and practical wisdom deal with things that are variable. Nor are these first principles the objects of philosophic wisdom, for it is a mark of the philosopher to have *demonstration* about some things. If, then, the states of mind by which we have truth and are never deceived about things invariable or even variable are scientific knowledge, practical wisdom, philosophic wisdom, and intuitive reason, and it cannot be any of the three (i.e., practical wisdom, scientific knowledge, or philosophic wisdom), the remaining alternative is that it is *intuitive reason* that grasps the first principles."

Aristotle's conjunction of practical experience, contemplation, universality, necessity, justice, wisdom and happiness can only, we repeat, give rise to the most profound wonder and an uncommonly noble frame of mind. As Aristotle says in another passage from the *Nicomachean Ethics* (X, 7), "If happiness is activity in accordance with virtue, it is reasonable that it should be in accordance with

93

the highest virtue; and this will be that of the best thing in us. Whether it be reason or something else that is this element which is thought to be our natural ruler and guide and to take thought of things noble and divine, whether it be itself also divine or only the most divine element in us, the activity of this in accordance with its proper virtue will be perfect happiness."

*Erroneous Theories of an Immovable, Purely Intellectual Reason*. Ancient philosophy usually contrasted reason and feeling. Sensations and feelings were mobile, while reason was immobile and stable. A principle of mutability and becoming, thanks to which sensations provide pleasure, was always emphasized with regard to feeling. Reason, on the other hand, resembled a solid rock, so there could be no question of any bliss intrinsic to this rock. Such a view, which was widespread even beyond antiquity, does not at all apply to Aristotle and his philosophical theories, abstract as they may be. In a passage we shall presently quote, he demolishes the opposition between the two principles and finds process, and life, and pleasure, in reason. Here is where one must seek the attitude to the philosophy of reason characteristic of the Lyceum.

In the *Nicomachean Ethics* (VII, 11), Aristotle cites different opinions on what pleasure is and how, linked as it is to sense perceptions, it can correspond to the good. We read: "The reasons given for the view that pleasure is not a good at all are that every pleasure is a perceptible process to a natural state, and that no process is of the same kind as its end, e.g. no process of building of the same kind as a house. A temperate man avoids pleasures. A man of practical wisdom pursues what is free from pain, not what is pleasant. The pleasures are a hindrance to thought, and the more so the more one delights in them, e.g. in sexual pleasure; for no one could think of anything while absorbed in this. There is no art of pleasure; but every good is the product of some art. Children and the brutes pursue pleasures. The reasons for the view that not all pleasures are good are that there are pleasures that are actually base and objects of reproach, and there are harmful pleasures; for some pleasant things are unhealthy. The reason for the view that the best thing in the world is not pleasure is that

94

pleasure is not an end but a process." And so it appears that regardless of the differences of opinion as to whether pleasure should be viewed as a good or not, one thing is certain: it is something fluid, transitory, perceived only in process, as is natural for feelings and sensations but not for reason, devoid as it is of all variability and hence, of pleasure.

*Aristotle's Positive Teaching on the Identicalness of Reason, Happiness and Pleasure*. Not one of these views he presents suits Aristotle. The supreme good and supreme reason for him are not some dead immobile rock in comparison with which only sense experiences could afford pleasure. No, the abstract constructions of reason have their own attraction; and the more profound, the more detailed the work of reason, the more one attains the good and the sweeter, the more blissful is this good. Therefore the contemplative experiencing of all these reasonable and rational forms offers hope for their overall scrutiny, and the entire practice of detailed scientific analysis of an object does not exclude a contemplative attitude to it but, on the contrary, pure contemplation is precisely the blissful inclusion of all details, now bereft of all agitation and fuss. Hence in another part of the *Nicomachean Ethics* Aristotle arrives at this remarkable conclusion: "And we think happiness has pleasure mingled with it, but the activity of philosophic wisdom is admittedly the pleasantest of virtuous activities; at all events the pursuit of it is thought to offer pleasures marvellous for their purity and their enduringness, and it is to be expected that those who know will pass their time more pleasantly than those who inquire" (X, 7). This is quite natural, since knowledge of the ideas is beautiful. It is no wonder that Aristotle writes: "The apparent good is the object of appetite, and the real good is the primary object of rational wish" (*Metaphysics* XII, 7).

*All Philosophy Is Beauty*. Thus the philosophy of the Lyceum affirms the supreme abstraction of reason, sees a certain blissful sweetness lurking in it; however, the contemplation of reason and the loftiest abstract ideas does not exclude the practical pursuit of concrete, detailed, careful investigations; on the contrary, it is their blissful consummation and universalization. As we know, the state of bliss is far above all the goods and evils of everyday life. The philosophy of the Lyceum teaches one to strive for the ultimate good, or, which is one and the same, for eternal reason, which is the cause of all that is best. And Aristotle says, disputing the Pythagorean and Platonic philosophers: "Those who suppose, as the Pythagoreans and Speusippus do, that supreme beauty and goodness are not present in the beginning, because the beginnings both of plants and of animals are *causes*, but beauty and completeness are in the effects of these, are wrong in their opinion. For the seed comes from other individuals which are prior and complete, and the first thing is not seed but the complete being" (*Metaphysics* XII, 7). The supreme good is the source of everything, it is complete, beautiful and perfect.

Therefore in their understanding of philosophy the followers of Aristotle were not at all troubled by the presence of evil or ugliness since the supreme good, the beautiful and reasonable, is always opposed to them. From the rest of Aristotle's biography we shall see that all the dramatic complexities of life could not disturb his wisdom or thwart his endless patience, industriousness and faith in the victory of reason. Aristotle was convinced that truth was reached at the cost of great effort. But he well understood that there is another way of finding truth—through joint research and cooperation. He writes of this on several occasions, primarily in the treatises *On Sophistical Refutations* (34) and *Topics* (VI, 14).

In a word, all knowledge is beautiful according to Aristotle. All philosophy is true beauty, to which one must always give oneself up completely, endlessly, patiently, diligently, serenely, trusting in the possibility of achieving truth and beauty and, finally, without making any extravagant claims, but strictly separating what is intelligible to man from what is not. In the treatise *On the Parts of Animals* we read: "Of things constituted by nature some are ungenerated, imperishable, and eternal, while others are subject to generation and decay. The former are excellent beyond compare and divine, but less accessible to knowledge. The evidence that might throw light on them, and on the problems which we long to solve respecting them, is furnished but scantily by sensation; whereas respecting

perishable plants and animals we have abundant information, living as we do in their midst, and ample data may be
collected concerning all their various kinds, if only we are
willing to take sufficient pains. Both departments, however, have their special charm. The scanty conceptions to
which we can attain of celestial things give us, from their
excellence, more pleasure than all our knowledge of the
world in which we live: just as a half glimpse of persons
that we love is more delightful than a leisurely view of
other things, whatever their number and dimensions. On
the other hand, in certitude and in completeness our
knowledge of terrestrial things has the advantage. Moreover, their greater nearness and affinity to us balances
somewhat the loftier interest of the heavenly things that
are the objects of the higher philosophy" (I, 5).

*Science Is a Painstakingly Exact Investigation of Life.*
The followers of Aristotle were always distinguished for,
and even proud of, the strict scientificality of their thinking. These claims of the Peripatetics did not find much
favor in antiquity. Many people then, as now, were
troubled by the extraordinary laboriousness as it were of
these philosophers' mental explorations and their customary fondness for all sorts of minute investigations and
probing of trifling details, which is seen as an example of
some sort of scholasticism and casuistry. But this is not at
all correct.

Aristotle and his school always liked to study life both
at its source and in its external manifestations. But any
kind of life — and the cosmos was seen as universal life —
was always beautiful to Aristotle. In the same section of
the treatise just quoted from we read further: "We therefore must not recoil with childish aversion from the examination of the humbler animals. Every realm of nature is
marvellous ... we should venture on the study of every kind
of animal without distaste; for each and all will reveal to us
something natural and something beautiful. Absence of
haphazard and conduciveness of everything to an end are
to be found in Nature's works in the highest degree, and
the resultant end of her generations and combinations is a
form of the beautiful" (I, 5).

97

We shall cite a few examples of how Aristotle, for all the generalizing capacity of his mind, was endlessly interested in all sorts of trifles, details and facts, which sometimes bear relation to the universalizing constructions of his philosophy but sometimes are not related to them at all and are simply interesting to Aristotle in themselves. In such instances Aristotle is not only unafraid of dissipating his energies in his observations and descriptions, but on the contrary just loves to go off into endless details even about subjects of small importance to him.

Thus, in explaining how housekeeping should be set up, Aristotle writes in his *Aeconomica* (fragment 182) that a home is formed of four relationships—the father's to his children, the husband's to his wife, the master's to his servants, and income to expenditures, in such a way that expenses not be greater than income, for that is dissipation, nor income greater than expenses, for that is miserliness and baseness.

It would seem that family affairs of this sort are far removed from the thorough and detailed studies of a history of rhetoric. But Aristotle's encyclopedic mind was interested both in family questions and the history of rhetoric. According to Cicero, Aristotle collected, compared and joined together all the old writers dealing with the art of rhetoric. He wrote down the instructions of each with great care, elucidated the difficult passages and diligently expounded upon them. In so doing he so surpassed these first founders of rhetoric in the beauty and concision of his language that people no longer cared to acquaint themselves with their prescriptions in their own books, but all who wished to understand what their advice really amounted to turned to Aristotle's book as a much more convenient explanation (fragment 136).[14]

But if Aristotle entered so minutely into the historical issues of rhetoric, it is not surprising that in addressing Homer he tried to resolve some of the contradictions that arise when one reads his works. Why does Homer say in the *Odyssey* (XI, 634) that the head of the dreadful monster Gorgon is in Hades when the *Iliad* (V, 741) tells us that Athena bears it on her shield? Aristotle responds that the goddess did not at all have it on her shield, just as she did not have "Strife" or "horrible Onslaught withal" on it

98

either. The poet had in mind here only the horror evoked by the Gorgon, which was conveyed to those gazing upon the goddess' aegis (fragment 153).

Further on Aristotle takes up the question of why Ajax told the Trojan Hector of Achilles' wrath and unwillingness to join in battle, thus opening the way for the Trojans' onslaught. After all there was no need for such step, and besides a reasonable man should not inform his enemies of his side's calamities. Aristotle untangles this seeming illogicality: Ajax had to proclaim Achilles' wrath, otherwise Hector would have thought that Achilles did not enter the fray out of cowardice; but Hector had to know that Achilles and the other Achaeans were stronger than he (fragment 157).

"And the tall spears are planted by their sides," says Homer (*Iliad* III, 135). But it is bad to thrust spear-shafts into the ground; and if one of the spears thus planted should fall down at night it would make a lot of noise. Aristotle explains this seemingly strange expression as follows: in his poetry Homer always depicted what was the practice in his day, and in those ancient times the Greeks did as the Barbarians still do; many Barbarians thus plant their spears (fragment 160).

"Therewith the goddess spread a table with ambrosia and set it by him, and mixed the ruddy nectar," says Homer of the nymph Calypso (*Odyssey* V, 90). If the gods drink nothing but nectar, why did Calypso give some to Hermes "mixed"? For if she mixed it with water, then they drink water as well as nectar. Aristotle resolves the confusion in this way: the word translated as "mix" (*cerasai*) can mean either "to mix one liquid with another" or simply "to pour", for the word has both these meanings; and in the phrase "mixed the ruddy nectar" it in fact means not to mix but merely to pour (fragment 170).

Sometimes Aristotle gets too bogged down in historical facts and their diversity even begins to hinder his critical judgment, as one can ascertain from his appraisal of the Pythagoreans. In his account he tells of miraculous occurrences in the life of Pythagoras, for example, how a god greeted Pythagoras by name (fragment 191), and relays the ancient division of all living beings into gods, people and creatures like Pythagoras (fragment 192). On the other hand, he provides various sobering facts about Pythagoras: for example the Pythagoreans actually did eat meat except for certain parts of animals, which they declined for symbolic reasons (fragment 194): not eating the heart symbolically meant not tormenting oneself with sorrow (fragment 197). Aristotle pedantically enumerates lists of Pythagorean symbols, showing there is nothing mysterious about them: not stepping over a yoke meant not getting carried away by money-making; not raking coals with a knife meant not irritating a choleric person; not plucking at wreaths, not defiling the laws of the state, for the laws crown the state so to speak (fragment 197).

Aristotle's encyclopedic concerns are truly unending. He was interested in the problem of the flooding of the Nile (fragment 246) and established that its floods were caused by rainfall in its mountain sources. To this end, he asked Alexander the Great to send people there to ascertain the reasons for the flooding by direct observation. The problem was cleared up for Aristotle since the floods were patently shown to be caused by rainfall.

In his *Physical Problems* (fragments 210-244), Aristotle touches on the phases of the moon, the reason it is harmful to drink melted snow, why it is worse to wash clothes in salt water, why white wine is less inebriating than red, how the heat of the sun is transmitted to ripening fruit, why people blush with shame and pale with fear. He was also interested in weather prognosis based on the direction of the wind and the behavior of birds and animals.[15]

Overall Aristotle is amazing for his extraordinary love of nature study, his tireless observation and recording of all kinds of rare and sometimes even amusing phenomena.

In a discussion of swans and doves Aelian cited Aristotle as saying that swans are notable for the quantity and beauty of their young as well as their belligerence, for they are often roused into a fury against each other and get into fights in which they kill each other; Aristotle also said that sometimes they even battled with eagles, though in self-defence and not initiating the fight. Aelian goes on to say that swans are commonly famed for their singing, although he has not heard them sing and thinks that perhaps nobody has but that everyone accepts on faith that they do and that their song is particularly beautiful and mellifluous before death; swans can fly across the open sea and also along the shore without tiring their wings (I, 14).

Aristotle also wrote books on metals, plants and agriculture, where he describes countless particulars about these subjects in equal detail.

Amidst all this diversity of often haphazard information one comes across ideas that are strikingly correct and well-grounded. Meditating on the starry sky, Aristotle writes: "Our observations of the stars make it evident, not only that the earth is circular, but also that it is a circle of no great size. For quite a small change of position to south or north causes a manifest alteration of the horizon. There is much change, I mean, in the stars which are overhead, and the stars seen are different, as one moves northward or southward. Indeed there are some stars seen in Egypt and in the neighborhood of Cyprus which are not seen in the northerly regions; and stars, which in the north are never beyond the range of observation, in those regions rise and set. All of which goes to show not only that the earth is circular in shape, but also that it is a sphere of no great size" (*On the Heavens* II, 14).

Elsewhere Aristotle described the customs and institutions of nearly all the Barbarian as well as the Greek states. One life of Aristotle affirms that he followed Alexander the Great to the Brahmins of India and that his observations of the habits of many countries allowed him to describe 255 types of government. He wrote a book entitled *The Customs of Barbarians*, as well as a book on the claims and rights of the Greek city-states, on the history of the Pythian games with a list of the victors and one or even several books called *Peplos* ("The Garment"), containing a variety of materials, from a list of national Greek sports competitions to a collection of epitaphs from the graves of ancient heroes.

Such was Aristotle's attitude to philosophy, and to all other sciences as well, as it found expression at the Lyceum. One cannot fail to note his infinite devotion to both major and minor areas of philosophy, his patience in the process of searching out the truth, his conception of all existence as life, as well as his tranquillity and greatness of spirit before all types of evil and outrage, which he felt did not hinder the ultimate victory of truth, goodness and beauty but only confirmed the existence of these lofty spheres. One must especially keep all this in mind when reviewing the dismal circumstances which seemingly triumphed in the philosopher's last days.

It is not surprising that in his will Aristotle's disciple Theophrastus instructed that the bust of Aristotle be placed in the shrine of the Muses along with the rest of the dedicated offerings (Diogenes Laertius V, 51).

## Aristotle's Letters

Interested in the most diverse sciences, the natural sciences no less than the humanities, as well as different types of art from both ideological and formal points of view, Aristotle was also directly engaged in literature himself, particularly poetry. At the beginning of this book we already had occasion to say that Aristotle was far from pursuing only abstract constructs and that he was also the author of a number of poetic works. Some letters, known as Aristotle's in antiquity, have also come down to us; from them we can assess his epistolary skill. At that time the art of letter-writing was valued no less than the art of eloquence, since a letter was the same sort of conversation with another, and revealed the personality, frame of mind and thoughts of those who were exchanging epistles.

*Extension of Aristotle's Encyclopedism to his Literary Art.* The fact that Aristotle engaged in writing poetry of his own alongside his work in the natural sciences, medicine, biology, rhetoric and history of the theater only confirms his encyclopedic propensities. His surviving poems, for instance the verses glorifying Plato (which were mentioned earlier), or Hermeias (which will be discussed later), as well as his poetic prose glorifying the beauty of nature (which has also been cited earlier) give a sufficient idea of Aristotle's artistic inclinations. We shall now devote some time to his letters.

*The Epistolary Genre.* The outstanding rhetorician Demetrius the Cynic (first century AD) notes in his work *On Style* (IV, 230) that Aristotle was "exceptionally successful in attaining the epistolary manner".[16] He informs us that a certain Artemon, who probably collected and transcribed Aristotle's letters in the third century BC (although he may have composed them himself) claimed from the example of Aristotle's letters that "a letter ought to be written in the same manner as a dialogue" (IV, 223). However, Demetrius himself thought that Aristotle's letters sometimes turned into whole treatises although he personally felt that "the heightening should not, however, be carried so far that we have a treatise in place of a letter, as is the case with those of Aristotle to Alexander and with that of Plato to Dion's friends" (IV, 234). He also comments that "Aristotle, however, sometimes uses actual proofs, but in the way appropriate to a letter" (IV, 232).

Demetrius' remarks characterize the style of Aristotle's letters as being simple. But elsewhere he says that Aristotle's letters contain jokes, not of the kind that are more elevated and filled with dignity but of the sort that are more common and close to buffoonery (III, 163-165).

The elegance of Aristotle's epistolary style is noted in fragments 668 and 669, although sometimes his letters were written in the most simple language, very close to ordinary everyday and conversational speech.

The sources speak of the concision of Aristotle's letters, as well as of their broad intelligibility and originality. Aelius, one of the late commentators on Aristotle's *Categories,* wrote that in his private writings, his letters, Aristotle was terse and at the same time as easily understandable as he was original — understandable to anyone because his epistolary style did not differ from ordinary conversation, and original without falling into carelessness; yet he could be abrupt as well (fragment 667).

The abundance of Aristotle's letters, their varied style and their great fame will convert anyone who, having studied the philosopher's other writings, is in the habit of thinking that Aristotle's style is dry, hard to understand, monotonously abstract, devoid of all artistic elements, far from clear and simple, and always overly scholastic.

Ammonius Saccas, another late commentator of Aristotle, wrote that Aristotle was obviously a master of the epistolary style, which should be brief and clear and shun excessive dryness in the combination of phrases and expressions. Simplicius wrote that Aristotle's ability to express himself clearly was best demonstrated by the character of his letters, where, as befitted the epistolary style, he appropriately mimicked everyday conversation; none of the famous writers had a letter style comparable to Aristotle's.

Aristotle not only liked to write letters, but had an extremely varied and wide-ranging style, as Simplicius also attests. He tells us that some of Aristotle's works were classed as lectures (for instance his works on logic and physics), in the sense that he addressed them orally to his closest students; others were called familiar writings (these were the ones he wrote to his friends); still others were termed exoteric, and were in the form of letters to people who were not close to him, written at their request. The latter were also called "circular" works because on receipt those who had asked for them were to read them aloud in front of a group standing in a circle so that all could hear equally well. In these writings, when treating of divine matters, Aristotle would often demonstrate that the prime intellect is divine, is above everything and necessarily abides immutably in an unwavering sphere.

Many ancient authors felt that Aristotle's letters should not be disregarded or considered somehow incidental. In the view of the late writer Philoponus, Aristotle's letters were a very important area of his writings, no less than his theoretical treatises: he said that Aristotle's works were divided into those dealing with private matters, such as his letters, those dealing with general issues, such as the *Physics*, *On the Soul* and so forth, and those dealing with questions of an intermediate nature, such as his *Politics* and *Historia Animalium*; the personal ones were those he wrote to someone in particular, for instance his letters and all his answers to Alexander the Great's questions on ruling and how to establish colonies.

As for the content of his letters, we have already touched on it several times previously. They are notable for their great nobility of spirit and enormous concern for the needs of Greece as a whole. In concluding this section on Aristotle's letters we shall cite some materials we have not yet discussed.

*A Letter to Alexander.* Aristotle's letters to Alexander are striking first of all for their noble sentiments and attempt to defend the oppressed and appeal to the humane feelings of the Macedonian potentates. We shall describe one of them. Although some doubt its authenticity, it is indicative that a letter of the kind should have been linked with Aristotle's name. The letter states that many sages have proved that doing good gives one access to the lot of gods, because the life of humans rests on receiving gifts and giving them, consisting as it does in giving away, receiving and again giving forth. Therefore it is fine and just to show pity—for pity is a sign of a meek spirit, and cruelty, of an ill-bred one—and relieve all who are undeservedly unfortunate, and especially good people; for it is disgraceful and cruel to scorn virtue stricken by misfortune. Hence Aristotle approves of Theophrastus when he says that showing pity never leads to repentance. He tells Alexander to try to be prompt to do good and slow to anger, for the former is regal and merciful, while the latter is repulsive and befitting Barbarians. Finally, he urges Alexander to do as he thinks right without disdaining useful advice.

It would be hard to imagine a letter by a great philosopher distinguished by a loftier content and more pronounced humane feelings.


*A Letter to Theophrastus.* In this connection it is expedient to mention one other letter from Aristotle addressed to his student Theophrastus and marked by the same lofty temper. In it Aristotle says that sudden injustice is unquestionably better than injustice of long duration; for the memory of it and the harm it occasions last only a short time, while long-standing and deeply-rooted injustice creates eternal hatred; and reconciliation often follows the former after one kind word, whereas we can find no way out of the latter even after much agitation and torment. Therefore one should not behave unjustly with one's associates in the first place—there are no reasonable grounds for doing so—but if it is impossible to abstain, after one has unwillingly acted unfairly, one should rapidly put an end to the hatred. After all it is beyond human power to entirely refrain from injustice anyway; but repairing a blunder brings much good and is especially a feature of balanced minds.

*Sense of Equality with Kings.* It must be noted that in his letters to the sovereigns of the world of his day, Aristotle was not at all some pitiful and crude flatterer. While giving them various lofty admonitions, he felt on the same plane as they. An example of such a letter is the one cited by Plutarch which we mentioned earlier, although Plutarch is well known not to have been at all particular about the literal truth of the documents he cites. Let us remind our readers of a notable instance in Aristotle's correspondence with Alexander so that they can judge for themselves of the overall character of Aristotle's letters. Alexander, far off in Asia, was displeased that Aristotle had openly written about the truths which at one time he himself had considered esoteric, i.e., intended for a narrow circle of students. Since we have already quoted Alexander's letter on the subject, we shall here reproduce Aristotle's response, laconically self-possessed and full of dignity: "Aristotle to King Alexander, Greeting. You have written to me regarding my acroatic lectures, thinking that I ought to have kept them secret. Know then that they have both been made public and not made public. For they are intelligible only to those who have heard me. Farewell, King Alexander."[17]

*Realistic Approach to Life.* Finally, Aristotle's letters are also full of a multitude of different facts reflecting the confused events of the time. For example, everyone usually knows that Aristotle asked King Philip to restore his native town of Stagira, which was located near the city of Olynthus he had destroyed. The king was not at all averse to granting Aristotle's request. But there were spies and informers about who got Philip not to restore Olynthus and to leave Stagira in ruins. Aristotle was critical-minded enough to see through these kinds of intrigues, but he could do nothing to aid his native town. This is what the late writer Dio Chrysostom has to say on the subject: "And I used to envy Aristotle at times because, being a native of Stagira—Stagira was a village in the territory of Olynthus—and having become the teacher of Alexander and an acquaintance of Philip's after the capture of Olynthus, he brought it about that Stagira was resettled, and they used to say that he alone had had the good fortune to become founder of his fatherland. But meanwhile, quite recently, I came upon a letter in which he exhibits a change of heart and laments, saying that some of these settlers are trying to corrupt, not only the king, but also the satraps who came there, so as to thwart any good outcome and to prevent entirely the resettlement of the city.

"But when some persons, exiles and homeless as they were, were actually annoyed by the prospect of having a fatherland and enjoying constitutional government in independence, but preferred to be scattered in villages like Barbarians rather than to have the form and name of a city, would it be proper, I ask you, to feel surprise no matter what else annoys certain persons? Accordingly, just as Aristotle has written in his letter as one who has become sick and tired of his troubles — for he says he is holding up his fingers — you may consider that I too am holding up my own fingers, as well as any other fingers there are. For in truth the infatuation of those fellows proved more than a match for the exertions of Aristotle, so that they did not permit the petty village to grow to the rank of a city, and to this day the spot is uninhabited" ("The Forty-Seventh Discourse" 9-11).

In summing up Aristotle's epistolary legacy, it must be said that Aristotle was an outstanding composer of letters. He wrote so many of them that in antiquity they were classed as a special section of his works, like the division comprising his great theoretical writings. Moreover, Aristotle used the most diverse styles in his letters, ranging from language close to that of scholarly treatises to the diction of lively conversation, jokes and everyday speech. We have spoken of the clarity of his letters, their intelligibility and popular style that had nothing in common with the difficult texts of his major philosophical works, and even of the elegance of his epistolary style.

And in general the obscurity, dryness and abstractness of Aristotle's philosophical treatises are usually greatly exaggerated. To explain difficult ideas Aristotle often gives the most simple examples, intelligible even to an ill-educated person. He almost never uses new, unprecedented or complicated terminology, although he is literally enamored of the most subtle theoretical discourses and the inexorable logic of thought. He is sometimes very difficult to read and requires concentrated attention.

But at the same time Aristotle unexpectedly emerges as a true artist of the word. Cicero, for one, remarked on the obscurity of his language. But also none understood better than Cicero the profundity of Aristotle's artistic devices when he spoke of his golden flow of eloquence and the unbelievable sweetness and richness of his language, as well as the "ornate style" of Plato, Aristotle and Theophrastus (*Orator* XIX, 62).

Reading Aristotle, one senses that he is speaking to a whole auditorium, trying to explain every detail and by no means pronouncing categorical judgments. His speech is filled with all kinds of suppositions, conjectures, of searching after what is not understood, establishing the probability of this or that argument, of repetitions of what he has already said and of elucidations.

The content of Aristotle's letters is quite heterogeneous, almost always noble, and attests to his courage and lofty human sentiments. Indications of all kinds of intrigues and squabbling surrounding the philosopher are also not lacking in his letters. But if we said previously that Aristotle is the outstanding encyclopedist of the ancient world, this judgment applies not only to his theoretical philosophy, but also to his everyday interests, refers to his cheerful and courageous attitude to surrounding reality. Aristotle loved pure thinking in all its most abstract constructions. But he also loved life, loved playing a big role in it and by nature happily combined theoretical purposefulness and a very active political spirit. But this is where Aristotle collided with the tragedy of life and ended up being vanquished despite all his philosophical wisdom and his everyday practicality. We shall see as much when we turn to the great philosopher's last years.

### NOTES

[1]The second-century AD Roman writer Saint Justin Martyr claims that Aristotle tutored Alexander for only five years altogether.

[2]The Attic talent was a great sum of money in Aristotle's day.

[3]*The Complete Works of Homer*, p. 156.

[4]The etymology of the Greek word *lyceum* is rather interesting. Most often it is said to be derived from the root *lyc, which is at the basis of the word *lycos*, or "wolf". In ancient times the gods were pictured in the form of animals. Apollo Lycius (in Asia Minor) and Zeus Lycius (in Athens) were worshipped in the guise of a wolf. This conception was reinterpreted, and the gods became the protectors of humans, who destroyed wolves, i.e., Wolf-Slayers. The word *lyceum* is also held to be derived from the Greek word *leycos*, or "light", "white", related to the Latin *lux*, "light". Over the course of the millennia zoomorphic and light-related conceptions of the gods alternated, succeeded each other and even fused. The word *lyceum* is thus very ancient. Today it is used to refer to an educational establishment, sometimes of a privileged type.

[5]Xenophon, "Hipparchicus, or a Treatise on the Duties of a Commander of Cavalry" (3, 1), *Xenophon's Minor Works*, George Bell and Sons, London, 1878, pp. 309, 310.

[6]Xenophon, *Hellenica* [History of Greece] (I, 1, 33), Harvard University Press, Cambridge, 1947, p. 15.

[7]Greek *peripateo*: to walk around, stroll.

[8]As quoted in Athenaeus, "Deipnosophistae" (VIII, 354b), *The Deipnosophists in 7 Volumes*, William Heinemann Ltd., London, 1930, 4: 103-05.

[9]Cicero, "Academica II" (112, 131), *Cicero in 28 Volumes*, 19: 611, 637.

[10]Pliny, *Natural History in 10 Volumes* (VIII, 17, 44), William Heinemann Ltd., London, 1947, 3: 35.

[11]Plato, "Parmenides" (129a-135d), *Dialogues of Plato*, pp. 487-91.

[12]*The Great, and Eudemian, Ethics, the Politics, and Economics, of Aristotle*, Manor Place, London, 1811, pp. 116-19.

[13]*Aristotle in 23 Volumes,* Harvard University Press, Cambridge, 1977, 18: 469-75, 587-615.

[14]Cicero, *Orator* (XXXII, 114; LI, 172; LVII, 192, 194, 196; LXIV, 218; LXVII, 228).

[15]*Aristotle in 23 Volumes*, 15: 859-930.

[16]Demetrius, "On Style" (IV, 230), in *Aristotle in 23 Volumes*, 23: 443.

[17]As quoted in Aulus Gellius, *The Attic Nights in 3 Volumes* (XX, V, 12), 3: 435.

# VI

## Aristotle's Last Years

Of particular importance for understanding Aristotle's last years is his connection with Alexander the Great. Aristotle left the Macedonian court to come to Athens but did not break off his very close ties with Alexander, whose generosity and attention to Aristotle's scholarly research, as we have said, greatly helped him in his position as head of the Lyceum. But in spite of their intimacy, Aristotle and Alexander's relations were far from easy.

Let us say a few words about Aristotle's differences with Alexander. They were not much to speak of, although the reasons for them were serious enough. In the first place Aristotle did not much approve of Alexander's constant campaigns since he advocated more spiritual occupations in life, and Alexander himself had had a sufficiently thorough schooling under Aristotle not to regret the impossibility of pursuing his study on account of his distant and difficult military campaigns.

As a typical child of Greek culture, Aristotle hated and feared any kind of tyranny. It is remarkable that people subsequently affirmed that he had even been a party to Alexander's poisoning.

### The Question of Alexander's Poisoning by Aristotle

In his biography of Alexander, Plutarch lists a great many names linked with rumors of Alexander's poisoning (ch. 77). The rumor originated, incidentally, with King Antigonus, a former military commander of Alexander's who at first ruled over part of Asia Minor and later on over Syria as well. The question is discussed by such prominent ancient historians and writers as Pliny, Arrian, Dion Cassius and the twelfth-century Byzantine historian

Zonaras. It was indeed said that the poison had been sent by Antipater at Aristotle's advice, and the properties of the poison, which was supposedly prepared for Alexander at Aristotle's urging, were even described: "They say, heard King Antigonus speak of it, and tell us that the poison was water, deadly cold as ice, distilled from a rock in the district of Nonacris [in Arcadia], which they gathered like a thin dew, and kept in an ass's hoof; for it was so very cold and penetrating that no other vessel would hold it" (Plutarch, *The Lives of the Noble Grecians and Romans.— Alexander*, p. 576). One cannot entirely ignore all such rumors of Alexander's poisoning which circulated in antiquity, although Plutarch believes that most writers of the day regarded the whole thing as a fabrication.

We admittedly find ourselves in a very difficult position here. Not to credit in the slightest such serious writers as Pliny the Elder, Arrian or Dion Cassius is quite impossible. On the other hand, the enormity of Aristotle's poisoning Alexander puts us on our guard and makes us call into question the truth of such information.

Aristotle was, apart from everything else, a physician and a botanist, and to whom could such prescriptions for poisoning more aptly be attributed? All these considerations leave one with a very unpleasant feeling of inconclusiveness, when it is impossible to say simply yes or no. Some monstrous story is unquestionably hidden here. But what is it?

History, alas, knows of only too many great people who have combined genius and villainy.

Finally, even if one deems these reports to be pure invention, the matter is still not altogether simple. Some historians and philologists say that such a fabrication could well have had a very real political meaning, since Alexander's heirs were deeply at odds and could invent the most unbelievable calumnies against each other. Probably this kind of slander concerning Alexander's poisoning at Aristotle's advice was thought up by certain successors of Alexander against others whom Aristotle might have sympathized with. Apart from that, subsequent Aristotelians might have blackened Alexander because of his reprisal against Aristotle's nephew Callisthenes, and in revenge their opponents might have imputed to Aristotle involve-

111

ment in a crime. However, all these versions are most likely conjecture and rumors, which the ancient world abounded in where great people were concerned.

Yet there were also serious disagreements between Aristotle and Alexander, among them differences concerning Alexander's policies in the East.

## Concerning the Greeks and the Barbarians

The fact is that in spite of the breadth of his philosophical views, Aristotle remained a typical Greek to the end of his life, not acknowledging the Barbarians to be real people and deeply respecting ancient Greek customs. As for Alexander, despite his great esteem for all that was Greek, he never could admit the Barbarians to be devoid of human dignity. To the contrary, he even considered it his historical mission to unite the Greeks and Barbarians in one whole. This is what Plutarch has to say on the subject: "For Alexander did not follow Aristotle's advice to treat the Greeks as if he were their leader, and other peoples as if he were their master; to have regard for the Greeks as for friends and kindred, but to conduct himself toward other peoples as though they were plants or animals; for to do so would have been to cumber his leadership with numerous battles and banishments and festering seditions. But, as he believed that he came as a heaven-sent governor to all, and as a mediator for the whole world, those whom he could not persuade to unite with him, he conquered by force of arms, and he brought together into one body all men everywhere, uniting and mixing into one great loving-cup, as it were, men's lives, their characters, their marriages, their very habits of life. He bade them all consider as their fatherland the whole inhabited earth, as their stronghold and protection his camp, as akin to them all good men, and as foreigners only the wicked; they should not distinguish between Grecian and foreigner by Grecian cloak and targe, or scimitar and jacket; but the distinguishing mark of the Grecian should be seen in virtue, and that of the foreigner in iniquity; clothing and food, marriage and manner of life they

112

should regard as common to all, being blended into one by ties of blood and children."[1]

All these differences between Aristotle and Alexander on national and political issues were further complicated by the fact that Alexander, so to speak, implemented Greco-Barbarian unity in his own personal life. As if it were not enough that he once saw to it that thirty thousand Barbarian boys be taught to read and write in Greek and wield Macedonian weapons, he also behaved provocatively in the sense that he got married to several women from foreign, so-called Barbarian tribes. In Bactria, a northern province of Persia, he caused great devastation, destroyed fortresses, executed commanders. But at the same time, wishing to express a complete internal alliance between Macedonia and the Barbarians, he hastily married the Bactrian woman Roxana. According to Plutarch, "His marriage to Roxana, whom he saw in her youthful beauty taking part in a dance at a banquet, was a love affair, and yet it was thought to harmonize well with the matters which he had in hand. For the Barbarians were encouraged by the partnership into which the marriage brought them, and they were beyond measure fond of Alexander, because, most temperate of all men that he was in these matters, he would not consent to approach even the only woman who ever mastered his affections, without the sanction of law."[2] Later on Alexander married Stateira, daughter of the Persian king Darius III. This marriage began sumptuously, because at the same time Alexander celebrated the marriage of his companions, assigning the noblest women to his noblest men, and gave a general wedding feast for those of his Macedonians who had already contracted other marriages. At this feast, we are told, nine thousand guests reclined at supper, to each of whom a golden cup for the libations was given. All the other appointments, too, were amazingly splendid, and the host paid himself the debts which his guests owed, the whole outlay amounting to nine thousand eight hundred and seventy talents (ibid., 70, pp. 419-21).

But that was only the beginning. And this is how the whole business ended: when Alexander died, Roxana was pregnant; "but she was jealous of Stateira, and therefore deceived her by a forged letter into coming where she was, and when she had got her there, slew her, together with her sister, threw their bodies into the well, and filled the well with earth" (ibid., 77, p. 437).

After such goings-on, how could Aristotle, a Greek through and through and traditional opponent of any kind of barbarity, have regarded Alexander? Amazingly enough, despite such behavior on Alexander's part the relationship between him and Aristotle, though it may have dimmed somewhat, remained fundamentally intact. The two great men still continued to communicate. Even an episode that was frankly painful to Aristotle did not destroy their friendship.

## The Killing of Callisthenes

Alexander, as we know, was a very hot-tempered man, and in the last years of his life a suspicious one as well. When his friend Clitus strongly objected to the introduction at court of customs observed by oriental despots, he was so infuriated that he snatched up a spear and killed Clitus on the spot. Alexander himself suffered more than anyone from his deed. He sobbed all night over it, and nobody could calm him. Then Anaxarchus, a follower of Democritus, and Aristotle's relative Callisthenes were brought in to him. Aristotle had sent Callisthenes to Alexander's camp as his secretary and chronicler of his military campaigns, presumably with loyal intentions.

Callisthenes was a native of the city of Olynthus, a former Athenian colony. Thrice in 349 BC Olynthus had asked for the Athenians' help against Philip. But Athens was too weak. To win over the inhabitants of Olynthus, Philip even gave them neighboring Potidaea. But they still continued to resist him, and Olynthus was captured by Philip in 348 BC only thanks to traitors within the city, where a pro-Macedonian group was active. The city was razed to its foundations. At that time Callisthenes was around twenty. He was not only a relative, but also a great admirer of Aristotle, who had raised his nephew himself. Callisthenes evidently accompanied Aristotle to his friend and patron Hermeias of Atarneus. And when Aristotle was forced to move to Lesbos on account of the dangerous

114

situation in Atarneus, Callisthenes again came along. Apparently even after Aristotle's departure for Macedonia Callisthenes remained with him and continued to be his student, as was at that same time Theophrastus, for instance, Aristotle's future successor at the Lyceum. It is specifically known that Aristotle tutored Callisthenes in history, inculcated in him a love for Thucydides, and on the whole made him a highly educated historian and rhetorician. For some time Callisthenes was Aristotle's secretary and helped him compose historical works.

Aristotle and Callisthenes parted only in 335 BC, when Aristotle returned to Athens for good. Callisthenes remained with Alexander, whose school companion he had been under Aristotle. But even after Aristotle's departure for Athens Callisthenes did not lose touch with him, sending his teacher various scientific materials, particularly of a zoological nature. For his part Aristotle hoped to maintain his ties with Alexander through Callisthenes. Callisthenes behaved rather freely at court. It was said that he got the king to restore his native Olynthus, destroyed by Philip. It is true, however, that after Philip's capture of Olynthus Callisthenes could hardly have felt much respect for the Macedonians. In any event, his too familiar behavior at the court provoked Aristotle's censure. The historian Arrian frankly accuses Callisthenes of rudeness.

Let us now return to the Clitus episode. How did Anaxarchus and Callisthenes comfort Alexander when they came to him?

The severe and harsh Anaxarchus began to put Alexander to shame for his paltry and slavish bearing in grief, which he said was not at all worthy of a king. And this somewhat consoled Alexander.

As for Callisthenes, on this occasion he addressed the king very mildly and affectionately. However, Alexander was not overfond of Callisthenes, who did not hesitate to rebuke him, and quite severely. At the same time Callisthenes' intimacy with the king and his irreproachable reputation aroused great envy.

And the time came when Alexander began to consider Callisthenes his enemy.

When once at a banquet Callisthenes had made a brilliant speech in defence of Macedonia at the king's request, so that all who were present not only applauded but threw their wreaths at him, the king then ordered him to utter a speech against the Macedonians. And Callisthenes pronounced it with such ardor that Alexander felt him to be his most dangerous enemy. He said that Callisthenes had shown not so much the force of his eloquence as the force of his hatred for Macedonians. Alexander's malevolent feelings intensified still further because on leaving the feast Callisthenes several times repeated on his account Homer's famous phrase, "Patroklos too is dead, who was better far than thou" (*Iliad* XXI, 107), an allusion to the fact that Alexander, too, was mortal if better heroes than he had died.

On learning of this sort of behavior, Aristotle said that Callisthenes was a fine orator, but a foolish man. Not only did Callisthenes refuse to fall face downward in front of the king as was the custom in the East, he even tried to convince him to renounce such homage. Once at a banquet when all Alexander's retainers fell face downward before him and then went up to kiss him, Callisthenes directly went up to kiss the king, who angrily turned away.

Such actions aroused the hatred not only of the king but also of many of his attendants, who slanderously began to accuse Callisthenes of inciting the youth against the king. Therefore when a plot of young Macedonians against Alexander was disclosed in 327 BC, and when none of the conspirators, even under frightful torture, named Callisthenes as a participant in or organizer of the plot, Alexander did not yet execute the philosopher, but already announced that he would punish not only Callisthenes but also those who had sent him to him and those who received conspirators against the king in their cities. In his threats Alexander was undoubtedly alluding to Aristotle. There were varying reports of Callisthenes' death (in the spring of 327 BC). Some said that Alexander had ordered him to be hanged, others, that he had died after suffering greatly in prison for seven months.

It goes without saying that Callisthenes' fate could not fail to dampen the friendly relations between Aristotle and Alexander.

True enough, there is no concrete information about Aristotle's reaction to Callisthenes' death, although he was personally told of it by someone who came from Alexander's camp. But it is quite possible that persistent rumors arose back in antiquity about Aristotle's participation in Alexander's poisoning on account of Callisthenes. The news of Callisthenes' death spread all over Greece – that much is clear.

The whole tragedy of these decades in the history of Greece was that the overwhelming majority of the Greek population continued to live according to the old democratic ideals of Pericles. Absolutely everyone in ancient Greece, first among them Plato and Aristotle, condemned tyranny. Since Alexander was deemed Aristotle's pupil, many prominent figures of the time, particularly in pro-Macedonian circles, cherished the hope that Alexander would prove an enlightened monarch striving to unite the whole of fragmented Greece on the basis of a rational and humane state system. The death of Callisthenes stripped the Greeks of all illusions concerning the enlightened and humane nature of Alexander's power and made them see the king as an oriental despot, cruel and inhuman, securing his power through endless bloody crimes. Callisthenes became a martyr who had given his life for freedom and human dignity, which not so long ago, at the time of the Greco-Persian wars, had prevailed over bloody, immoral and barbaric eastern tyranny. After Callisthenes' death all Greek illusions concerning Macedonian dominion disappeared once and for all. If anyone still continued to extol Alexander and his successors, it was only out of pusillanimity.

In his comparative live-stories of illustrious Greek and Roman public figures written four centuries after Aristotle's death, Plutarch excelled in remaining faithful to the old Greek ideals of enlightenment while maintaining a laudatory attitude toward the Romans, who in spite of having learned much from the Greeks, nevertheless were regarded by the latter as typical Barbarians. This is why Callisthenes' fate helps to rightly estimate the enlightened Greek scholar's attitude to Macedonian despotism.

## Politics and Morals

There were other factors which could not but contribute to Alexander's estrangement from Aristotle, creating a noticeable cooling between teacher and pupil. Thus, one of King Philip's retainers, Antipater, had a son named Cassander. On account of his distant campaigns, Alexander appointed Antipater ruler of Macedonia and Greece. But Alexander's attitude toward Antipater was scarcely one of goodwill. All sorts of rumors and gossip and even outright calumny circulated against Antipater. Cassander would defend his father against all the false accusations in the presence of Alexander, who feared a plot on Antipater's part. Once the king irritatedly said that Antipater and Cassander would pay dearly for Aristotle's sophisms (Plutarch, *Alexander* 74), thus indirectly accusing the philosopher of wiliness and cunning.

In fact Plutarch writes: "later, however, he held him [Aristotle] in more or less of suspicion, not to the extent of doing him any harm" (ibid., VIII, 3). It was not only a question of the two men's personal relations. Aristotle undoubtedly realized what the fall of the free Greek city-states would lead to and what Macedonian rule would bring. His misgivings led him to address letters not only to Alexander but even to Philip, with all kinds of moral admonitions and sometimes direct requests for mercy toward Greece.

One such letter to Philip has come down to us in which Aristotle says that those who assume leadership and perform good deeds for their subjects not by chance but by their own nature derive boldness, not from relying on possessions, which are perishable, but take pride only in their virtues and their ability to be a good and prudent citizen; for there is nothing stable and firm in the world of men, and even the sun lasts only until evening: the first vicissitude destroys, changes and muddles all human lives. Therefore Philip should not try to act with drastic bravery or to treat the Greeks more tyrannically, but to be a benefactor to them; for the former is the sign of rashness, while tyranny is frankly ill-advised. Reasonable rulers should not be marvelled at for their domains but their domains should marvel at them, so that after a reversal of fortune they would be worthy of the same praise. Aristotle concluded the letter by wishing Philip prosperity and telling him to direct his soul toward philosophy and his body toward health.

118

As we know, Aristotle wrote moralizing letters to Alexander as well. In one such missive he said that he did not know what force drew him to Alexander; whatever came to mind, everything in him seemed great and remarkable, and Aristotle saw nothing worthy of oblivion but only what deserved remembrance and encouragement. Time could dim nothing here, because fine counsels and admonitions have eternity as their spectator. He therefore urged Alexander to turn his power not into arrogance but into good deeds befitting virtue, beyond which there is nothing in life. Man, mortal by nature, can after inevitable death win himself eternal memory thanks to the greatness of his deeds. Aristotle then told Alexander to remember that he had not been brought up foolishly like some people, who acquire ridiculous convictions; he was of noble origin, had an inherited kingdom, a reliable education and universal fame. And to the same degree as he was distinguished by the gifts of fortune should he be preeminent in valor and fine deeds. Aristotle ended his letter by exhorting Alexander to do useful deeds while completing what he had planned.

But Aristotle did not merely write the Macedonian kings moral admonitions in the most general and abstract sense. For he himself was a product of Greece and loved his country so much that he tried as far as possible to mitigate the Macedonian domination, which he unwillingly recognized as necessary. Another earlier letter written to Philip has been preserved in which Aristotle told him to withdraw his garrisons from the cities and give the Hellenes free rule, to allow those who were deluded to repent and immediately provide the right-minded with gifts; if he acted thus, and not once but always, he would preserve in the most reliable way the edifice of his power.

## Aristotle's Nationalistic Inclinations

Aristotle's cosmopolitanism and humanitarianism should not be exaggerated. The age-old Greek opposition of Greeks and Barbarians was typical of him as well. In his view the Greeks were real people. As for the non-Greeks, we already know that Aristotle frankly considered them the living beings bereft of reason.

Here, however, we must dwell on another important question, namely Aristotle's assessment of various nations. If we omit various trifles and concentrate on what is most important, we are struck both by the breadth of his views and by his purely Greek sympathies. In his *Politics* he writes: "Those who live in a cold climate and in Europe are full of spirit, but wanting in intelligence and skill; and therefore they retain comparative freedom, but have no political organization, and are incapable of ruling over others. Whereas the natives of Asia are intelligent and inventive, but they are wanting in spirit, and therefore they are always in a state of subjection and slavery. But the Hellenic race, which is situated between them, is likewise intermediate in character, being high-spirited and also intelligent. Hence it continues free, and is the best-governed of any nation, and, if it could be formed into one state, would be able to rule the world" (VII, 7).

Let's examine this evaluation in more detail, since it contains both many negative and some quite important positive features.

In the first place, Aristotle had too little historical material and first-hand observation in general to assess the peoples of the north, and hence ascribed to them only one quality which he could fully understand, namely the quality befitting peoples compelled to struggle for their existence in a harsh climate. Aristotle indeed had some grounds to speak of the spirit and courage of these northern peoples. On the whole, his opinion of the north can be accounted for only by the childish state of historical scholarship at the time; and who could have assessed the north as a definite cultural and historical entity in the fourth century BC?

Aristotle's appraisal of the Asians is a bit more realistic since the cultural and historical life of Asia was known to him in more detail. But here, too, reducing the whole of the Orient to simple slavery, while reserving its peoples a proclivity for the arts and sciences, would be regarded as naive today. There were no more and no less arts and sciences in the East than in the West. As for a "state of subjection and slavery", the ancient Orient may indeed have been more notable for these qualities than Europe as represented by ancient Greece, which early on began to manifest quite definite germs of democratic thinking, which blossomed forth in Athens.

But what is truly indubitable is the Greeks' great courage and spirit and at the same time enormous propensity for the arts and sciences.

Aristotle was quite familiar with the history of Greece and was a very intelligent socio-historical observer in general. The combination of strength and beauty in the popular ethos of Greece could not fail to strike him. And he could speak loudly and openly of this amazing unity, backing himself with thousands of well-known facts.

Finally, the extent to which the political unity of the Greek people had been weakened by fragmentation did not escape Aristotle. Each city in Greece, even small ones, claimed independent and entirely separate statehood. Ancient Greece was not one big state. Only the *polis* could be a state, a city in which everyone knew everyone else, saw what anyone else was doing, where any undertaking was discussed and carried out jointly on the spot. The passage from Aristotle's *Politics* quoted above indicates that such a fragmented country can flourish only under a serious and intelligent leader.

### Aristotle's Attitude to Alexander

In many respects Aristotle could see such a person in Alexander. But there was no way he could imagine Alexander to be some absolute ideal. He knew well all the intrigues at the Macedonian court and all its gory horrors. As we shall see below, Philip had already made a mess of both his state and personal affairs and was killed by his own favorite Pausanias. Alexander himself shed the blood of his intimates on several occasions, and did it more out of ambition than for reasons of state. He was an intelligent and educated man who had indeed learned much from Aristotle and appreciated the arts and sciences. But he drank a lot, especially in his last years, and died after a few drunken nights. In his treatise *On Duty*, Cicero asserts: "Philip, king of Macedon, I observe, however surpassed by his son in achievements and fame, was superior to him in affability and refinement."[3] No sooner did Alexander die than discord broke out among his grandees and mutiny among his troops, joined by the destruction of his household and the fall of the state he had created with such great labor. Aristotle could not fail to have known all this and therefore he hardly idealized Alexander. We shall say nothing of the latter's edginess, hysteria and cruelty.

Without doubt, Alexander also had too high an opinion of himself. In his treatise *On Tranquillity of Mind* (13, 472e), Plutarch, wishing to say that even ordinary people can have true notions concerning the gods, cites a letter from Aristotle to Antipater where the philosopher contrasts these ordinary people with their right to be proud specifically to Alexander, who was proud because he ruled over many men.[4] In this letter Aristotle is expressing the thought that communing with the gods is in no way a function of ruling over a large number of people, as Alexander did, but is quite possible without such government.

Here we face the very difficult historical question of Aristotle's attitude to Alexander. Aristotle was undoubtedly astounded that Alexander declared himself a god because the priest of the Egyptian god Ammon-Ra (whom the Greeks, incidentally, identified with Zeus-Helios) had told him that Ammon considered him his son. This proclamation was later followed by all sorts of divine homages paid the king. But let us not be too surprised at such worship.

It must be borne in mind that in antiquity the Greeks did not see an impassable abyss between humans and gods. In ancient mythology we find frequent transformations of gods into people and people into gods. Take, for example, the well-known hero Heracles, who was said to be in Hades after his death but at the same time, according to legend, had been admitted into the assembly of Olympic gods for all eternity and lived on Olympus. The young Ganymede, a Trojan princeling beloved by Zeus, was abducted by his eagle and also ended up on Olympus. Eos the goddess of dawn immortalized Tithonus, another son of the Trojan king, after entering into marriage with him.

Even in historic times the practice of hero-worship was also quite developed in Greece. An outstanding person was declared a hero after his death, i.e., even if he was not a god he was at any event honored as a demigod. With the huge development of culture and civilization in the classical period of Greece, deification and hero-worship became rarer, although the great dramatist Sophocles, for one, was declared such a heroic demigod.

But behold an extraordinary phenomenon on the Greek horizon – the world dominion of a single sovereign, Alexander. It was unquestionably a social and historical necessity, since as a result of the growth of productive forces the small, isolated city-states of the classical period could no longer make do with the closed, isolated structure characteristic of the old Greek cities. At the time of Alexander's conquests the need arose for a state which could firmly unite the countries he had conquered, scattered as they were over enormous expanses, and Greece with her *polises*. Alexander's empire sprang up, and it made a tremendous impression on the people of his day. One must understand these people who, finding themselves in the presence of an omnipotent and omnipresent sovereign, fell on their faces before him, fearing to perish momentarily at his slightest whim. One can comprehend Alexander's restoration of the ancient cults of the East, where the Egyptian pharaoh, for example, was seriously believed to be either the son of a god or a god himself.

One can find traces of the deification of a conqueror of the world even during Philip's reign. Already at that time in Macedonia triumphal processions were held in which not only representations of the twelve Olympic gods were carried but a thirteenth figure as well, that of Philip, who was termed the altarmate of the gods.

Proclaiming Alexander the son of Ammon in Egypt was linked with a whole series of miraculous events, so the sources tell us. On their way to the temple, Alexander and his companions traversed a desert. But Zeus sent abundant rains, which cooled the scorching sand, making it moist and hard, and cleared the air, so that it became easy to breathe. Then when it turned out that the markers set up to help guides had been destroyed and the Macedonians were wandering off track and losing each other, ravens suddenly appeared and began to show them the way. "Moreover, what was most astonishing of all, Callisthenes tells us that the birds by their cries called back those who straggled away in the night, and cawed until they had set them in the track of the march" (Plutarch, *Alexander* 27).

Plutarch makes another telling point: "It was difficult to turn him [Alexander] aside from any course so ever when he had once set out upon it. For Fortune, by yielding to his onsets, was making his purpose obstinate, and the high spirit which he carried into his undertakings rendered his ambition finally invincible, so that it subdued not only enemies, but even times and places" (*Alexander* 26).

Of course it was not only a question of Alexander's obstinacy, but also of the enormous political significance of the king's deification. Alexander had advanced through Asia Minor, taken Tyre, invaded Egypt and occupied Memphis. But it was not such a simple matter to get the better of Egypt. There was a famous oracle of the god Ammon-Ra, a priest who at Alexander's approach came to meet him and solemnly pronounced the will of the god. It is possible that Alexander did not initially have deification in mind but came to the famous oracle to confirm the necessity of his campaign against Persia and ascertain the Persians' participation in a plot against Philip. The oracle of Ammon did not provide Alexander with this second corroboration. On the other hand, it not only affirmed the necessity of the campaign against Persia but also proclaimed him a god just as Dionysus.

Alexander the Great did not realize his idea of a world empire. After his death the lands he had conquered quickly fell apart. Individual potentates were not loath to be called gods themselves. But already starting in the second century BC the Roman republic began to grow miraculously, and from the time of Augustus' reign in the late first century BC and early first century AD became a mighty empire, whose entire social and political life was permeated by the cult of the emperors. These were worshipped like real gods. Temples were built in their honor in which holy rituals were celebrated, sacrifices were made to them and incense was burned.

Thus if one surveys the history of the ancient world as a whole, Alexander's deification does not at all appear fantastic and unheard-of. Rather, it is part of the worship of all natural forces, the pantheistic orientation typical of antiquity.

Let us now examine the complex and uneasy political situation that reigned all over Greece in the second half of the fourth century BC as a result of Macedonian pressure. Only then will we get a clear picture of the socio-political environment in which Aristotle was fated to part with all his earthly joys and sufferings.

## Greece and Macedonia in the Second Half of the Fourth Century BC

If we were to review in detail the military and political activities of King Philip II of Macedonia, our heads would spin with the hundreds and thousands of large and small enterprises he undertook to take possession of Greece: conspiracies, intrigues, bribes, squabbles, political assassinations, open agreements, direct military action, betrayal. It is important to note that by the mid-fourth century BC two hostile parties had formed in Greece—an anti-Macedonian and a pro-Macedonian one.

This whole period in the history of Greece is one of constant conflicts, bitter fights to the death between the anti-Macedonian party, which stood for the full freedom of the ancient Greek cities, and the pro-Macedonian party, which deemed it best to submit to Macedonia.

In 346 BC in one of his speeches the famous Greek orator and patriot Demosthenes painted a picture of the sad state of the country which instead of heroically resisting Philip had fallen into utter decay as a result of petty disagreements and disputes between individual cities or politicians. Almost at the same time, in 344 BC, Isocrates, another famous orator and patriot with a completely different understanding of patriotism, openly called upon Philip to head Greece against the Persians. The no-less-famous orator Aeschines, who favored Macedonia, accused the anti-Macedonians, including Demosthenes, of having been bribed by the Persians to attack Philip. In general, Persian money was often of enormous importance in the military and political history of Greece. For instance, the Peloponnesian War, which had lasted for several decades at the close of the fifth century BC, ended to the advantage of the Spartans against the Athenians only thanks to Persian bribes.

What was Aristotle's position in the troubled last thirty years of the fourth century BC in Greece?

On the one hand, he naturally opposed the internal disintegration of Greece and supported the idea of Greeks' unification. He even considered this possible only under a single ruler for all of Greece, realizing that it was weakened by fragmentation into a multitude of separate city-states, each of which considered itself an integral, indivisible state inferior to no other in anything.

But could Aristotle recognize the Macedonian kings as the autocratic rulers of Greece? Hardly. He was all too familiar with the gory intrigues at the court of Philip and Alexander. If we say that in this troubled time Aristotle got confused, we shall not be far wrong.

The situation grew particularly complicated after Philip's assassination in 336 BC. In 338 BC Philip gained a victory over Athens and won many people to his side because his conditions for peace were very moderate. Through skilful maneuvering Philip included Athens in an all-Greek union and became its head. Furthermore, he announced it was the common task of the Greeks to undertake a campaign against Persia, and to subjugate this ancient enemy of theirs was an age-old dream of the Greeks. But an unexpected event occurred.

In the fall of 336 BC Philip planned to marry off his daughter from his first marriage to Olympias. A year earlier he had obtained a divorce from Olympias, Alexander's mother, and married Cleopatra, the niece of Attalus, one of his most powerful commanders. A certain youth named Pausanias, one of Philip's bodyguards, who had been insulted by Attalus and not backed up by Philip, decided to kill the king at his daughter's wedding and carried out his intention. Thus the great Philip perished most miserably. His death aroused new hopes in those Greeks who still dreamed of liberating their country from Macedonian domination and restoring free Greece.

The extraordinary drama of these events may be judged by the way Demosthenes, who had recognized the supremacy of Macedonia in 337 BC when Philip had seized all of Greece, now, after his death, triumphantly appeared before the popular assembly with the news of the Macedonian ruler's assassination. But Demosthenes' hopes for an anti-Macedonian insurrection were based on his naive confidence in the weakness of the youthful Alexander, whom he called a boy and a simpleton. But Alexander dealt quite energetically with a rebellion in Thebes, after which there were almost no more anti-Macedonian uprisings in Greece up to his death.

However, when in 336 BC Aeschines tried to obtain Demosthenes' conviction in court, he was not able to gather even a fifth of the necessary votes. But Demosthenes himself was already more cautious, not wishing to spoil relations with Alexander unnecessarily. When Alexander's treasurer Harpalus fled from him and arrived in Athens with a fleet and money, calling upon the city to revolt against Macedonia, Demosthenes not only did not support him but even suggested arresting him and turning him over to Alexander. Nevertheless, when the detained Harpalus escaped, Demosthenes and a number of other political figures who had been known for their anti-Macedonian sentiments were accused of complicity, and Demosthenes went into exile.

But after Alexander's death in 323 BC there was a new wave of anti-Macedonian uprisings in Greece. Demosthenes returned to Athens and was shown great honor. But his triumph was short-lived. The uprisings were suppressed, and the old political order of Solon's time (early sixth century BC) was reinstituted in Athens. Demosthenes went into hiding in the temple of Poseidon on the island of Calauria, where he was found by the volunteer "hunter of fugitives" Archias with a detachment of spearsmen. Demosthenes committed suicide by swallowing a strong poison.

The orator Hyperides, a student of Plato and Isocrates, was close to Demosthenes in his political views and shared a similar fate. He spoke out against Macedonia after Philip's death and miraculously escaped being turned over to his enemies. After Alexander's death, he, like other anti-Macedonian Greeks, took part in the struggle to free Greece. This struggle, as we know, proved unsuccessful: in Thessaly at the battle of Lamia in 322 BC the Greeks were routed by the seventy-eight-year-old Antipater, who had been a general already under Philip and had then served Alexander. After the defeat Hyperides fled to the island of Aegina, where he hid in the temple of Aecus, dedicated to the hero Ajax, along with Aristonicus and Himeraeus, his companions in the struggle. All three were seized and executed by order of Antipater.

Even Aeschines, the long-time defender of Macedonian hegemony, did not fare well either: after his failure in the trial of Demosthenes in 336 BC, he withdrew from political life and went into voluntary exile on the island of Rhodes, where he died in obscurity.

One can well imagine the difficult and tangled situation Aristotle found himself in after his arrival in Athens from Macedonia in 335 BC. As we have seen, his departure from the Academy for the north had already been hard to explain as motivated merely by philosophical considerations or the death of Plato. Philip's destruction of Stagira in 349 BC and of Olynthus in 348 BC was apparently of much greater significance. It would have been quite dangerous at that point for somebody close to the Macedonians to remain in Greece and make himself out to be a Greek patriot. It was better to leave, as Aristotle in fact did, heading north in 347 BC with the hope of influencing the Macedonian government.

In Macedonia Aristotle became the kings' intimate advisor and the defender of his beloved Greece. He was undoubtedly close to Philip and still had enough weight with Alexander to influence him in his treatment of Greece. It is at his insistence that Olynthus and Stagira were restored, and at his request after the battle of Chaeronea in 338 BC that Philip spared Athens, although many other Greek cities were razed to the ground. In 335 BC Aristotle came to Athens not for the sake of a pleasant trip to the land of philosophers and poets, but undoubtedly for serious political purposes. Some contemporary historians said outright that he had come to Athens as a person invested with Alexander's and Antipater's political trust and secretly acting in the interest of Macedonia.

This probably explains the Athenians' contradictory attitude to Aristotle. On the one hand, a medieval Arab biography of Aristotle reports about a decree of the Athenian popular assembly to erect a column in Aristotle's honor with a highly respectful inscription where Aristotle was proclaimed almost the savior of Athens. On the other hand, the dyed-in-the-wool Greek patriots, always overflowing with anti-Macedonian sentiment, saw Aristotle as an enemy and found little to rejoice about in his return to Athens, which they viewed as hypocritical. But since open conflict with Aristotle was impossible in view of growing Macedonian power, a trial against him could be instituted only after Alexander's death in 323 BC, and even so this trial was conceived not as a political but as a religious one. The priest Eurymedon, according to Diogenes Laertius (V, 5-7), accused Aristotle of impiety, as a result of which, as we shall see, Aristotle was forced to flee from Athens to Euboea.[5] It is clear that the underlying motivation for the charge was not so much a religious as a political one. There was no impiety on Aristotle's part. It was only an excuse to settle accounts with a prominent Macedonian sympathizer with the help of accusations that would sound sufficiently weighty for the uninformed population.

It seems to us that one can see clear in all this mess only in the following way. On account of his political sympathies Aristotle was an alien in the Greek environment. The Greek patriots naturally perceived him as a secret if not open enemy, with whom they had to square accounts. On the other hand, Aristotle was linked to Macedonia only by place of birth. He was so firmly linked to Greek culture, knew and loved Greece, its past and present, so much, that he could in no way have been its enemy or a secret agent and spy for its enemies. Aristotle dreamed only of unifying fragmented and weakened Greece into one mighty and united nation, and it seemed to him that the Macedonian rulers could further this end.

Yet after witnessing countless bloody doings at the Macedonian court and the criminally aggressive politics of the Macedonian kings toward Greece, knowing of their preparations for conquering the Orient and opposing Alexander's Persian campaigns, Aristotle turned into a critic of Macedonian autocracy and in fact proved much more of

129

an adversary of the Macedonians than the Greek patriots, for he constantly made use of his high connections to push the kings toward a more humane and solicitous treatment of Greece.

In the end even illusions as to his influence vanished in him who had been considered a committed supporter of the power hostile to Athens. And so it was not surprising that rumors sprang up of Alexander being poisoned by Aristotle.

Such an interpretation of Aristotle's political loyalties clarifies the frustrating historical riddle in which contradictory Greek sources envelop Aristotle. In spite of everything, Aristotle was and remained a true Greek and, thrust into bloody political chaos, he lived and worked only for Greece. He was compelled to give up his Macedonian dreams since the Macedonian kings proved to be bloodthirsty conquerors.

### Flight from Athens

Soon after Alexander's death Aristotle left Athens for the neighboring island of Euboea and settled there in the city of Chalcis. If Strabo says that it was a comfortable, pleasant and undisturbed abode for philosophers (X, 1, 11), such a motive can hardly be taken seriously in determining the reasons for Aristotle's coming there. Otherwise one would have to conclude that Aristotle went there during the stormy events following Alexander's death simply in order to rest in solitude. A number of authors such as Justin and Procopius claim that Aristotle traveled to Euboea for scientific purposes, specifically to study the tides and currents of the Euboean Sea (a so-called euripus channel). Such motivation for Aristotle's departure to Chalcis also seems too weak.

A third version involves much more serious issues. As we mentioned above, Diogenes Laertius recounts that a high-ranking priest Eurymedon (or Demophilus) instituted proceedings against Aristotle, accusing him of impiety. What sacrilege was this that entailed such serious consequences? It turns out that "the ground of the charge [was] the hymn he composed to the aforesaid Hermeias, as

130

well as the following inscription for his statue at Delphi: 'This man in violation of the hallowed law of the immortals was unrighteously slain by the king of the bow-bearing Persians, who overcame him, not openly with a spear in murderous combat, but by treachery with the aid of one in whom he trusted'" (V, 5-6).

The reader no doubt remembers that Hermeias was the Platonic philosopher who ruled Atarneus, took in Aristotle and Xenocrates after their departure from Plato's Academy and was soon afterwards cruelly put to death by the Persians.

It is not quite clear why such devout verses were taken to be impious. Aristotle's enemies said that he had not simply extolled Hermeias as a man but deified him by writing a hymn in the spirit of the paeans which were usually addressed to Apollo.

This was all the more true of Aristotle's other poems honoring Hermeias, his accusers asserted. Diogenes Laertius also cites this hymn commemorating the slain ruler: "O virtue, toilsome for the generation of mortals to achieve, the fairest prize that life can win, for thy beauty, O virgin, it were a doom glorious in Hellas even to die and to endure fierce, untiring labors. Such courage dost thou implant in the mind, imperishable, better than gold, dearer than parents or soft-eyed sleep. For thy sake Heracles, son of Zeus, and the sons of Leda endured much in the tasks whereby they pursued thy might. And yearning after thee came Achilles and Ajax to the house of Hades, and for the sake of thy dear form the nursling of Atarneus too was bereft of the light of the sun. Therefore shall his deeds be sung, and the Muses, the daughters of Memory, shall make him immortal, exalting the majesty of Zeus, guardian of strangers, and the grace of lasting friendship" (V, 7-8).

Of interest is one other account which provides additional details on Aristotle's indictment and flight to Chalcis. The little-known writer Ptolemy of the early Christian era informs us that one of the priests called hierophants by the name of Eurymedon accused Aristotle of impiety for not worshipping the idols which were honored at the time; he did so out of hatred for the philosopher, as Aristotle said in a letter to Antipater. When Aristotle learned of this charge, he left Athens for his native Chalcis so as not

131

to cause the Athenians the same disasters they earned for killing Socrates (fragment 18).

The unjustly accused Aristotle is thus ranked with Socrates, who in 399 BC was also accused of impiety, of spurning the universally recognized gods and worshipping some new divinities, and of corrupting the youth. Socrates was forced to take poison, submitting to the verdict of the judges and Athenian law. But Aristotle was not Socrates and did not want to reconcile himself to obvious slander, so he secretly left Athens. His accusers had made use of a tried-and-true method, although the fantastic nature of the case was patent. Aristotle had met Hermeias in 347 BC and they had soon had to part. Hermeias was killed in 341 BC, and Aristotle was accused of impiety only in 323 BC, i.e., nearly twenty years after Hermeias' death. Moreover it was utterly implausible to see in Aristotle's verses a hymn worthy only of a divinity. The accuser's judgments in this case were exclusively subjective and prejudiced.

It seems to us that under the guise of impiety Aristotle was being charged by the Athenian democrats dreaming of restoring the former free Greece after the death of Alexander. It may also be possible that Diogenes Laertius is not telling the full story here or simply does not know it, or perhaps is confused, the more so as he is very prone to historical muddles.

Many ancient writers speak quite categorically of the socio-political underpinning of Aristotle's persecution by the Greek religious zealots at the end of his life. We shall cite only Aelian, who writes that having fled Athens for fear of a trial, Aristotle, in response to somebody's question as to what Athens was like, answered, alluding to the sycophants, magnificent, but pear upon pear grows old there and apple on apple, and fig upon fig[6]; when he was then asked why he had left Athens, he replied that he did not want his fellow-citizens to sin twice against philosophy, having in mind Socrates' death and the same danger threatening him (III, 36). Once again we find a reference to Socrates, who in his day was also accused of impiety. The frightful death sentence in his case too was explained by religious motives, as we know.

As Socrates once had, Aristotle also wrote a speech in his defence in which, according to the late Greek writer

Athenaeus, "if the speech is not a forgery", he logically proved the absurdity of the accusation: "If my purpose had been to sacrifice to Hermeias as a god, I should never have built for him the monument as for a mortal, nor, if I had wished to make him into the nature of a god, should I have honored his body with funeral rites" (fragment 645, *The Deipnosophists* XV, 679a).

Thus Aristotle's social and political situation was most complicated and troubled in 323 BC.

The great philosopher felt uneasy in those tangled circumstances. The Macedonians could not trust him, nor could the Greek democrats. He needed to flee to a place where he could safely devote himself to philosophy and continue his Lyceum pursuits, which he had abandoned for good. But where could he flee? Demosthenes, Hyperides and other leaders of the Greek struggle for independence had been forced to go into hiding, but then the only way for them to escape execution had proved to be death. Can one therefore be surprised at the existence of ancient accounts claiming that Aristotle died on Euboea after taking poison?

### The Poisoning of Alexander and Aristotle's Suicide

One should probably not totally disregard the reports that Aristotle, who had very problematic relations with the Athenian patriots as well as the Macedonian rulers, poisoned not only Alexander but himself as well with aconite, as Diogenes Laertius informs us (V, 8). In ancient mythology Hecate, the goddess of sorcery and the underworld, had taught the princess of Colchis Medea, also a sorceress, to brew poison out of herbs and flowers, and was believed to have discovered the poisonous properties of aconite (cf. Diodorus Siculus, historian of the first century BC). In the East, particularly in India, the tips of arrows to be used in battle were smeared with aconite. But through a certain process aconite becomes a medicinal, pain-killing agent. Having practised medicine all his life, Aristotle could not fail to know the properties of this plant. Nonetheless the story of Aristotle's suicide is recounted in various sources, including the twelfth-century Byzantine com-

133

mentator Eustathius Macrembolites and the Italian humanist of the fourteenth and fifteenth centuries Leonardo Aretino. Consequently, the tale persisted right up to the Renaissance.

We won't go after historical effects. But there evidently was something enigmatic about Aristotle's death. And whether he drank some aconite as a medicine to relieve stomach pains (for Aristotle had a stomach ailment) or whether he took a large dose to settle his accounts with life, the secret will always remain sealed.

Diogenes Laertius is considered by many to be a rather authoritative source for knowledge about the ancient philosophers. But he evidently vacillates on the question of Aristotle's suicide, referring himself to the historian Eumelus, according to whom the suicide supposedly took place. He does not mention the third-century BC Aristotelian Hermippus, who as far as we can judge from surviving reports, liked to discuss philosophers' suicides while gathering facts for their biographies. It may be that Diogenes Laertius borrowed his verdict on Aristotle's suicide from this Hermippus, although in this instance he says nothing about him.

One can nevertheless affirm, it seems, that many more historians wrote of Aristotle's natural death than disputed it. Very important and authoritative ancient sources speak definitely of Aristotle's natural death: Apollodorus, a historian, rhetorician and grammarian of the second century BC (incidentally, Diogenes Laertius also refers to him in counterpoise to his basic view), Dionysius of Halicarnassus, a rhetorician and historian of the first century BC, and Censorinus, a grammarian of the third century AD.

Various doubts and conjectures concerning both Alexander's poisoning and Aristotle's suicide are possible in view of the contradictoriness of the sources. Yet in reviewing the philosopher's last years we see that there were very solid grounds for Alexander's poisoning by Aristotle and Aristotle's own suicide, although these two events remain on the level of hypotheses.

It must not be forgotten that Aristotle's philosophy was to a high degree one of action and courage. Not without reason did Aristotle himself declare: "If you take away from a living being action, and still more production, what is left but contemplation?" (*Nicomachean Ethics* X, 8). But Aristotle could not be satisfied with merely contemplating philosophical ideas. He had to act. It was not at all in the spirit of the great Aristotle to reach despair and stop at that. The supposed fact that he had undertaken to fight a despot and wanted to poison him was considered as great an exploit as in its time the assassination of the notorious Greek tyrant Hipparchus at the pan-Athenian festival in 514 BC by the youths Harmodius and Aristogiton. Throughout antiquity Harmodius and Aristogiton were glorified as true patriots who had delivered the Greeks from slavery. Statues were erected to them and poets hymned them.

If we take an objective approach, we cannot deny the testimony of a number of ancient authors to Alexander's poisoning by Aristotle, just as we cannot conclusively reject the reports of Aristotle's suicide. If these events truly took place, they are quite justified by the dramatic circumstances of the philosopher's last years.

### Aristotle's Will

We have yet to discuss Aristotle's testament, in which he expresses his last will. The text of it is found in Diogenes Laertius (V, 11-16). Scholars who have studied it drawing on various other sources, generally conclude that in this case Diogenes Laertius' version is plausible enough and corresponds to Aristotle's life principles. The will is brief and businesslike. It is supposed that other versions which have not been preserved were more detailed.

The first thing that strikes the eye is that Aristotle named Antipater as his main executor. Whatever one may say of Aristotle's moods in the last days of his life, it is clear that pro-Macedonian sentiments to some degree or other still flickered in the heart of one who had once been close to the Macedonian kings, both father and son. True, Antipater as Alexander's viceroy and successor in Greece was too highly placed for Aristotle to be able to entrust him directly with executing his will. Therefore he designated a few more persons who were to see to it that his last will was carried out. At the same time he made his nephew Nicanor, the son of his sister Arimnesta, his true executor. Apparently at the time Aristotle drew up the will Nicanor was not at hand. But from the text of the document it is quite clear that Nicanor was extremely close to Aristotle and the report of his adoption by Aristotle may well be true.

In his testament Aristotle instructs that his daughter from his first wife Pythias, also named Pythias, be married to Nicanor.

He also reveals very warm feelings for both his first wife Pythias and his second wife Herpyllis. He instructs the ashes of his first wife to be moved to the same place where his would lie. As for Herpyllis, he put at her disposal either the house of his mother in Chalcis, where he had fled from Athens in 323 BC, or his father's house in Stagira. From this it is evident that at the time the will was drawn up Stagira had been sufficiently restored for Aristotle to continue to own his father's house. It appears, too, that Aristotle was a rather wealthy person with a few houses in different towns. Aristotle also did not object to the remarriage of Herpyllis, who was much younger than he. He only wanted her new husband to be a worthy man. Aristotle instructed that Herpyllis be given a talent of silver and, wherever she should live, that her dwelling be adequately furnished.

A little boy whose parents were unknown was being brought up in Aristotle's household. He also showed solicitude for this boy, entrusting him to Nicanor's care.

Aristotle gives very important directions concerning the slaves who lived with him and his relatives. Some he orders to be kept until a certain time, others are to be freed immediately, still others are to be freed before they reach a certain age.

Finally, this document reveals a very noble character of its author. He ordered statues to be erected to his nephew Nicanor, his guardian Proxenus, his brother Arimnestus and sister Arimnesta, and willed the statue of his mother to be dedicated to Demeter at Nemea. He also left instructions for stone sculptures to be erected to Zeus the Savior and Athena the Savior in thanksgiving for the safe return of Nicanor, who had often carried out important political missions for the Macedonian rulers.

The overall impression of Aristotle one gets from this will is of a man who was not only sensible and practical, but also very noble, kind and eager for peaceable and friendly relations among people, all this at a time when political, national, selfishly ambitious, cruel passions seethed around him. Nonetheless he invariably believed that "in all things the good is in the highest degree a principle"; and it is he who declared: "the world refuses to be governed badly" (*Metaphysics* XII, 10).

## NOTES

[1] Plutarch, "On the Fortune of Alexander" (I, 6, 329b-d), *Plutarch's Moralia in 15 Volumes*, Harvard University Press, Cambridge, 1962, 4: 397-99.

[2] Plutarch, "Alexander" (47), *Plutarch's Lives in 11 Volumes*, Harvard University Press, Cambridge, 1949, 7: 359-61.

[3] Cicero, "De Officiis" (I, 26, 90), *Cicero in 28 Volumes*, 21: 93.

[4] Plutarch, "On Tranquillity of Mind", *Plutarch's Moralia in 15 Volumes*, 7: 213.

[5] Diogenes Laertius also cites Favorinus' opinion that it was Demophilus who accused Aristotle, or both of them together.

[6] In Athens figs were a symbol of denunciation, since at one time there had been special informers who saw to it that figs were not secretly taken out of Athens. This is the origin of the word *sycophant*, i.e., figminder, the Greek word for fig being *sycon*. Favorinus cites Aristotle as saying that at Athens "pear upon pear grows old and fig upon fig" (as reported in Diogenes Laertius V, 9). This is paraphrase of the lines in the *Odyssey* describing the garden of king Alcinous, where "pear upon pear waxes old, and apple on apple, yea and cluster ripens upon cluster of the grape, and fig upon fig" (VII, 120).

# VII

## Aristotle's Philosophy

Aristotle's name in world literature is directly linked with Plato's. We have already indicated features Aristotle shared with his teacher Plato and points of divergence. But all our observations were made exclusively in connection with Aristotle's biography. Now in concluding our account it is necessary to speak at least briefly of Aristotle's philosophy as such and examine it as a whole distinct from Plato's philosophy. In so doing it must be kept in mind that great difficulties are encountered not only in understanding Aristotle's text itself, but also in the frequently distorted form it inevitably acquired at the hands of the numerous owners of his works, the scribes, interpreters, commentators and publishers who sometimes treated his words very arbitrarily. To present Aristotle from a contemporary point of view, we shall try to expound his philosophy as simply as possible, which is no easy task, particularly if one takes into consideration the great complexity and obscurity of his writings.

*1. If things really exist, then the ideas of things necessarily exist, so that without an idea the thing does not exist or the thing remains uncognizable.* Our starting-point is that the central category of Plato's philosophy, namely the Idea, or the *eidos* as it was called in Greek, was adopted almost entirely by Aristotle. If one understands this category in Plato, one will also basically comprehend the main principle of Aristotle's own philosophy, although he gave it a new interpretation.

Each thing, according to Plato, differs in some way from any other thing, therefore it possesses a number of essential properties, and the totality of all these essential properties of the thing is nothing other than the Idea of the thing. Indeed, denying the existence of the idea of a

138

thing in this sense would mean denying the existence of the thing itself as well, or at least would mean acknowledging it to be unknowable. If a thing really exists, it differs in some way from another thing; and if it differs in no way from anything, then it is not something at all, is not something about which one could say something. Thus the mere existence of a thing requires that it be the bearer of some idea. **On this point Plato and Aristotle are in complete agreement. Neither the one nor the other conceives of things without their ideas, their** *eidos*.

Let us continue. It immediately becomes clear that the idea of the thing also has a whole number of immaterial features. Thus, we breathe air, but we don't breathe the idea of air; if a person were to be put in an airless place, no idea of air in its pure form would save him from asphyxiation. Therefore the idea of the thing, which reflects and gives meaning to the thing, is not at all the substance itself which it actually reflects, but the meaning and essence of this substance. This is the sort of idea of things which was first advanced by Plato.

This was a discovery which astounded both Plato and his students. For there had been a time when people were unable to distinguish thinking from feeling. But then came the famous Greek philosopher Parmenides of the sixth and fifth centuries BC and discovered the difference, and even celebrated it in hymns filled with mythological symbols. There had been a time when people could not distinguish the numbers by means of which things are counted and calculated from the things themselves. But then came Pythagoras' school, which established that the number is not at all the thing itself, that things flow and change while the multiplication table always remains the same. And this discovery so struck people that they began to consider numbers divine and even equated them with the gods themselves. The very same thing happened with the concept of ideas. People suddenly realized that the idea of a thing is not at all the thing itself, but only its meaning and reflection. And this discovery, which today is clear and evident to anyone, was so enthusiastically proclaimed by Plato that he presented the ideas virtually as some divine essences. From our historical perspective we should understand the delight and amazement these discoveries evoked: let us not forget that they were all made two and a half thousand years ago.

*2. Aristotle criticizes the detachment of the idea of the thing from the thing itself.* But already Plato's closest adherents and pupils had found there was nothing at all divine about the ideas Plato had discovered. Plato was smart enough to realize the impossibility of fully separating the heavenly realm of the ideas from the most ordinary earthly things. After all, his theory of the Ideas had arisen only in trying to grasp what things were and whether it was possible to cognize them. Plato frequently said that the ideas of things can in no way be cut off from the things themselves, nowhere more clearly than in his most difficult and abstract dialogue, *Parmenides.* One must also realize that, carried away by the flow of his philosophical reasoning and his poetic exaggerations in expounding his views, Plato unwittingly separated and contrasted the beauty of the eternal ideas and the imperfection of the material world, giving a too abstract and remote-from-life description of the Ideas. Plato the exalted poet enamored of his realm of Ideas contradicted Plato the strict philosopher who understood the interdependence of idea and thing and their unity. This contradiction in Plato's theory gave occasion to Aristotle to break with him. Moreover, a school arose among Plato's pupils centered around the city of Megara whose members deepened the contradiction in Plato's thinking and began to preach the absolute isolation of the Idea of the thing from the thing itself, hence assuming a position of unconditional dualism.

Aristotle often heatedly attacks this conception of the isolated existence of the ideas. It is easy to see that he does not always specifically have Plato in mind, but rather these Megara philosophers who stood for absolute separation between the ideas of things and the things themselves. Aristotle's critical zeal was a philosophical exploit. **Even today in its criticism of the extremes of Platonic idealism, materialist philosophy leans on Aristotle's views.**

Yet one must remember that Aristotle did not himself deny the existence of ideas, but on the contrary did not conceive the world without them. He objected only to their separation and isolation from reality with all its infinite multitude and variety of things. The poetic raptures of Plato, who had sung the remote otherworldly realm of the beautiful ideas, were alien to the soberly reasoning Aristotle. But what Aristotle would put up with dealing with the entranced philosopher-poet he could not tolerate in those of his pupils who began systematically and consciously to affirm, with no longer any trace of poetry, the dualistic existence of the idea of the thing and the thing itself. Aristotle's criticism of this dualism was primarily directed against the one-sided vulgarization and simplification of Plato's theory of Ideas.

*3. The idea of the thing, according to Aristotle, is located within the thing itself.* What is the Aristotelian conception of the idea? **Aristotle conceives the idea of the thing to be not separate from the thing and off somewhere else, but within the thing itself.** For the idea of the thing is the essence of this thing. How can the essence of a thing be located outside the thing itself? And how can the idea of the thing be located in some other place, not influencing this thing and not giving it meaning and expressive form? The notion that the idea of the thing can be found in the thing itself does not at all contradict Platonism if the latter is sufficiently broadly conceived, and its logic and system fathomed.

Nevertheless Aristotelianism was a revolution with regard to Platonism which recognized the existence of a separate, heavenly world of ideas. Aristotle admitted that the idea of the thing could be anywhere, even outside the thing. However, whatever functions of the idea of the thing were involved, the most important for Aristotle was precisely the presence of the idea within the thing itself, the functioning of the idea of the thing within the thing itself, i.e., the complete absence of any gap between the two and of any dualism. **This thesis of the presence of the idea of the thing within the thing itself is the principal difference between Aristotelianism and Platonism.** Without this thesis everything else we are going to say here about Aristotle will become one-sided, not purely Aristotelian, and simply incorrect.

141

Now let us examine how Aristotle develops his theory of the ideas on the basis of his critique of the isolated existence of the ideas outside the things.

4. *The idea of the thing, being something individual, like the thing itself, is at the same time also a generalization of all of the parts of the thing, that is, a certain sum total.* First of all, although Aristotle stresses the existence of particularized ideas, the ideas for him are something fundamentally and necessarily general. **The idea of the thing, according to Aristotle, necessarily is an aggregate and universal of some kind.**

Indeed, any thing consists of its parts, whatever they may be. If we understand each such part to be fully isolated from the other parts of the thing and from the thing as a whole, it will be impossible to conceive what a part of the thing is. The part will end up being a kind of independent thing without any relation to the whole to which it belongs. In that case the whole would simply become fractioned into a number of independent things and cease being something integral. A part of a thing bears the entire thing as a whole; and if there are several such parts in the thing, then all of them express the integrity of the thing in different ways. We can speak of some part of a house, for example, of its individual rooms, hallways, living and auxiliary accommodations only if we know what a house is in general. A part of a house that is not generalized as the bearer, albeit only partial, of the idea of the house is in no way a part of the house. Likewise all the parts of a house are generalized in the whole which we call a house. A house taken as a mechanical and chaotic collection of parts is no house at all. A house always is this or that aggregate with which the individual parts of the house enter into relation and in light of which the parts of the house themselves interrelate.

Thus a house as a kind of idea, or the *eidos* of a house, always necessarily is some general aggregate to which the individual partial elements of that house are subordinated. Aristotle never tires of saying that scientific knowledge is possible only as science of the general and universal. If science studies only mutually isolated and totally ungeneralized objects, there is no science. Scientific thinking means generalizing. Remaining at the level of separate, mutually isolated, completely ungeneralized particulars means renouncing any science concerning these particulars, being left with only a blind perception of all the chaos of things and seeing no farther than one's own nose. This is not science but its total absence. However, not only the aggregation of parts within some one whole is important for scientific knowledge. If we take two, three or infinitely many things without generalizing them in any way, we will also remain outside science. Therefore the *eidos* **in all senses and respects is always a general aggregate or universal.**

Aristotle very clearly distinguishes both the universal from the particular and the necessary from the accidental. Scientific knowledge is possible only with regard to the general and universal, since all that is ungeneralized and mutually isolated is merely accidental. What is accidental is perceived by the senses and is always amorphous, so that there is no question here of any kind of necessity. If we were to find some regularity in the accidental, it would cease being an accidental to our thinking and would become a necessity, which in the form of some aggregate or universal comprehends all that is accidental, thus stripping it of senseless heterogeneity and complete unintelligibility. "Scientific knowledge and its object differ from opinion and the object of opinion in that scientific knowledge is commensurately universal and proceeds by necessary connexions, and that which is necessary cannot be otherwise... So though there are things which are true and real and yet can be otherwise" (*Posterior Analytics* I, 33). "There is no knowledge by demonstration of chance conjunctions; for chance conjunctions exist neither by necessity nor as general connexions but comprise what comes to be as something distinct from these" (ibid., I, 30, 20). Thus, **the idea, or eidos, is universal, necessary and equivalent to scientific law.** "Even if perception as a faculty is of 'the such' and not merely of a 'this somewhat', yet one must at any rate actually perceive a 'this somewhat', and at a definite present place and time: but that which is commensurately universal and true in all cases one cannot perceive, since it is not 'this' and it is not 'now'; if it were, it would not be commensurately universal—the

143

term we apply to what is always and everywhere" (ibid., I, 31, 30).

On the other hand, can we deal only with universals and can the idea, or *eidos*, be only a universal, excluding all particulars? After all, the *eidos* is a universal precisely because there are individual, particular elements whose generalization leads us to the *eidos*. For the universal always presupposes the presence within it of these or those particular things, whose generalization it actually is. If there is no particular, then no universal exists either.

Aristotle mercilessly criticizes the notion of universal ideas which have meaning all by themselves and presuppose no particular. **The *eidos* of a thing is not only the generalization of its individual elements. It necessarily is also something particular.** It is in its particularity that the given idea of a thing differs from all other ideas and, consequently, from all other things. However fragmented, chaotic and indefinite a thing may be, if it really is a thing, it necessarily is itself, i.e., something particular and, therefore, something *eidetic*, so to speak. The air can be cold or hot, dry or humid, clean or polluted, rarefied (as in the mountains) or dense, fresh or stuffy, and so forth and so on, but in all these cases it still is air, and not water or earth or stone or plant or animal, although all these objects can be found in it. The air is something, and consequently some one thing, and consequently some particular thing, and – if we grasp its meaning, or in other words its idea – something *eidetic*. The *eidos* of a thing is indivisible although the thing itself is divisible in infinitely many respects. Aristotle's argument in support of the *eidos* of the thing being something particular, located within the thing itself and not outside it is completely irrefutable; and if some followers of Plato recognized the ideas only as some general aggregates, forgetting their particular existence, there's no denying that Aristotle's criticism of such types of Platonism is justified.

5. *The totality of the thing necessarily exists in each individual part of the thing, and exists in a different way each time; but this means that the totality of the thing comprises all its separate parts and is therefore the integrity of the thing.* But the matter goes far beyond this train of reasoning. The

whole difficulty in studying any kind of things, both material and immaterial, is precisely that **it is utterly impossible to isolate the general from the particular and the particular from the general.** Take any material thing, a tree, say, or a stone, or a stream, or a knoll. We know that any thing is an indivisible sum of all its parts. And we also know that any thing is something particular or consists of particular things. In other words, the general and the particular must somehow be united into some one thing. Some peculiarity of the thing must be found wherein the general sum and the particular are indistinguishable. And in a remarkably concrete and rather intelligible manner Aristotle locates the indivisibility of the general and the particular in what he calls **the whole,** or **the integrity.**

The *eidos* **of the thing, being a certain general sum and a certain particular, is at the same time also a certain kind of an integral.** And in the integral whole the general and the particular indeed cannot be torn apart. If one removes some one element of a whole, it immediately ceases to be a whole. If you remove the hands from a watch, the watch instantly loses its integrity. If you remove the roof from a house (for instance to repair it), it ceases being a whole and, virtually speaking, being a house. A part of a whole can of course be examined separately from the whole whose part it is. And this isolated part of the whole will also be a whole, but no longer the same whole from which it was extracted. Naturally this or that beam which enters into the makeup of a hut's walls can be removed from it. But in that case, first, the hut will lose its integrity; while the beam removed from it will also be a whole, but this whole will no longer be a hut as something whole.

Thus, wherever we turn, there are always aggregates, there are always particulars and there are always integral wholes. In other words, all that exists is defined, shaped and knowable only because it is an *eidos* or at least contains its *eidos* within itself.

6. *The terms "idea", "eidos", "form", and "thing".* It is proper to note here that the Greek word *eidos* which Aristotle uses is traditionally translated by the Latin word *form*. There is some sense in such a translation because it

allows one to bring together as far as possible the *eidos* or idea of the thing and the thing itself and thus stress Aristotle's conception of the presence of the *eidos* of the thing within the thing itself. On the other hand, such a translation is quite incorrect because Plato calls an idea not only an "idea" but also an "*eidos*" (the two words being synonymous for him), both terms refer to vision, either sensory or mental, and both found universal dissemination thanks to the ancients' propensity to see everything with their own eyes and generally to perceive through the senses, in sensations. But Plato's terms "idea" and "*eidos*" are never translated by the word "form", in order to stress that Plato's Ideas are located outside the things. Therefore when Plato's philosophy is referred to as the doctrine of "ideas" and Aristotle's as the doctrine of "forms", great confusion is engendered in scholarship, since Plato's terms "idea" and "*eidos*" can also be rendered by the word "form" and Aristotle's "form" can be translated as "idea". Connecting "ideas" only with Plato and "forms" only with Aristotle is an attempt to establish at all costs the gap between Plato and Aristotle. While an abyss truly lay between them in some cases, in others there were quite strong and reliable bridges from one side of the abyss to the other. We shall not object to the use of the word "form" for Aristotle. But we must always remember that it is the very same thing as Plato's "idea" or "*eidos*", only with a special interpretation of all these terms.

7. *The integrity of the thing, where the whole thing perishes with the removal of one of its parts, is the organism of the thing, in contrast to the mechanism of the thing, where the thing remains integral despite the removal of individual parts of it and their replacement by other parts.* As we immerse ourselves further in Aristotle's theory of integralness, we come across a feature which though it may not always be distinctly enough articulated from a terminological point of view, nevertheless gives a quite specific coloring to his whole philosophy, so much so that it can be considered one of Aristotle's central categories, not only in his philosophy of nature, as it may appear at first glance, but in his entire world view.

146

The pertinent passages in Aristotle are very scattered, difficult and employ completely different terminology. Therefore, so as not to enter into all the philological difficulties surrounding this issue, we shall try to express it in our own words and, we hope, clearly.

Say we have before us some thing which presents itself as a whole. And say some part of this thing gets damaged, stops performing its function or even simply falls off. And say an expert comes who repairs this part of the thing and the thing begins to function as before. Thus, if the hands of a clock get broken or fall off, it is no trouble for a watchmaker to affix new hands, and the clock will fulfil its function as before. Nothing prevents us from damaging or even taking out a spring inside the clockworks, and the watchmaker from quickly restoring the clock to its former state.

But say we have before us another thing, such that the damage or destruction of one of its parts entails the destruction of that whole thing as well, after which it can no longer be restored. Say in the living organism of a person or any living creature, the heart, for instance, stopped functioning or was extracted in the course of some medical operation. This would prove to be not simply the destruction of the heart as a part of the organism but the destruction of the organism as a whole as well. Such is the case of the brain or the lungs. All these organs cannot be entirely removed from the organism and then restored by various artificial means, at least not in the present state of medicine. But what does this mean? It means that the heart or the lungs are vitally important for the whole organism in its entirety, embody integral being in all its substance, as philosophers would say. True enough, if one were to amputate an arm or a leg, the organism would continue to live. This means that not everything in the organism is organic in the absolute sense of the word. The organism may have other parts less essential to it which may mechanically be removed from it and mechanically replaced without any injury to the life of the organism as a whole.

We can now define an organism considered in its fundamental and specific form of existence and viewed in contrast to a mechanism. **An organism is that integral thing which has one or several parts in which the integral thing is present substantially.** Each individual thing, and

147

each individual living creature, and each individual historical era, and finally the whole universe in its entirety is such
an integral thing to Aristotle. This is not simply a sense
that the world is animate, which humans have always had
since primitive times. The entire mythology and, after all,
the entire poetry of the ancients is grounded in the animation of all that exists. With Aristotle it is not simply a question of nature and the universe being animate, but a carefully thought-out philosophical theory in which what is important is not the animation of the universe, which nobody
doubted in antiquity, but the **logical structure** requisite to
distinguish a mechanism from an organism and extend this
organicity to the entire cosmos.

*8. The four principles of the structure of any thing as an
organism. Form and matter.* Aristotle himself expounded
his theory of a thing as an organism many times and in
various ways. But it will probably be most expedient here
to describe what he himself calls "**the four causes**" or, as
we would say today, the four principles of any thing understood as an organism.

*The first principle* **is of course the** *eidos* **we spoke of earlier, without which one cannot understand one page of
Aristotle.** Remember that Aristotle uses this Platonic term
in a quite un-Platonic way. **The** *eidos* **of a thing is not at
all its otherworldly essence, but its essence located within
it, without which one cannot grasp what the given thing is.**
Aristotle very accurately calls this essence of the thing
"that which it is in itself". It is the "what" of the thing, i.e.,
the answer to the question of what this thing is. If we render Aristotle's term as the "whatness" of the thing, we
shall not be mistaken, although Aristotle understands this
"what" in a very profound and not at all everyday ordinary
sense. Every thing necessarily is something. Otherwise
there would not be that of whose properties we could
speak, i.e., the thing itself would not exist or at least would
remain unknowable. There is no animation here yet. But
there already is that of whose animation one can speak. In
expounding Aristotle, scholars usually call this principle of
definition of the thing its **formal principle.** But one can
make a big mistake if one does not keep in mind what we
said earlier about the *eidos*, idea and form of a thing. If we

148

understand these three terms to be completely identical we shall not be mistaken in speaking of Aristotle's formal principle. Properly speaking, it is an *eidetic* or **ideological, ideal, principle.** But on condition that we correctly, i.e., sufficiently broadly, understand the Aristotelian term "form", nothing prevents us from speaking of Aristotle's formal principle of the definition of existence.

*The second principle* we have also mentioned above, and said all that matters about it. But since we have undertaken to describe Aristotle's theory of the four principles of the structure of existence, we must devote special attention to this second principle here.

The fact is that matter and form constitute such a common and universally clear opposition that it would seem there is nothing to be said on the subject. The matter of this cupboard here is wood. And its form is the appearance assumed by the wooden materials processed for a definite purpose. It would seem there is nothing to ponder about here. And yet we are faced with one of the most profound issues in Aristotle's philosophy. Material for him is not at all simply material. For every material already has its own form. Is there any material which before being transformed into some object for human use does not have any shape at all? All the most formless, confused, disordered, chaotic things already have a form of their own. A pile of sand or lime even before being used in building a house already has a form of its own, namely the form of a pile. Clouds during a storm are also seemingly formless. But if a thundercloud really didn't have any shape, how could it be a cognizable thing for us? Rather, one might say that the matter of a thing is still only **the very possibility of its being shaped** and that this possibility is infinitely varied. Nevertheless, without matter the *eidos* would remain only the "whatness" of the thing, only its abstract meaning without any actual embodiment of this meaning in reality. The matter of a thing is its possibility, yet not an abstract possibility but the possibility of the very being of the thing. What the being of this thing is, the *eidos* embodied in it will tell us. On the other hand, the *eidos* itself without matter is also for the time being only the possibility of the thing, and not the thing itself. Only the complete union of the matter and *eidos* of a thing, or more

149

exactly only their complete identification makes the thing specifically the thing. I sit not on the matter of a bench, but on the bench itself. And I sit not on the *eidos* of the bench, but again on the bench itself. Philosophically speaking, the *eidos* of a thing is not its matter, nor is the matter of a thing its *eidos*. But once we have learned to distinguish the two, philosophical thinking requires us to recognize as well **the complete identity of the *eidos* and the matter of a thing.**

Plato had already distinguished the *eidos* and matter of a thing and didn't do a bad job of equating them either. But Aristotle's work in this area was almost a revolution with respect to Platonism. Of all the ancient philosophers who distinguished form from matter, Aristotle was the most profound and subtle at equating them. There is no question of naivete on Aristotle's part here. On the contrary, one should be amazed at the audacity of his philosophical discovery and his ability to think of form and matter as one and identical.

*9. Matter and chance. The causal and purposive principles.* In our very brief survey of Aristotle's theory of matter we deem it necessary to dwell on one more aspect, which will be most helpful in summing up Aristotle's philosophy as a whole. This aspect is the following.

**Matter is neither *eidos*, nor *eidos* in general, nor some *eidos* in particular.** Insofar as matter is only the possibility of the realization of the *eidos*, matter is the very fact of its realization, and an extra-*eidetic* fact, i.e., a fact outside meaning, since *eidos* is meaning. But what does this mean? It means that matter bears with it the **fortuitousness** of its realization, not envisaged by any *eidos*. Once we have overstepped the bounds of pure *eidos*, any extra-*eidetic* realization of the *eidos*, i.e., any realization outside meaning and hence even meaningless realization, is possible. The *eidos* can be realized in its entirety – and the matter will then become a principle of material beauty. But the *eidos* can also be realized not in its entirety, partially, contradictorily and even misshapenly – and the matter will then become a principle of material deformity. The integral realization of all the world ideas is a beautiful cosmos which is both utterly material, for we perceive it through our sensations, and utterly ideal, since the idea of the universe is fully embodied in it. But how is one to understand the partial and distorted realization of the *eidos*?

According to Aristotle, only the cosmic spheres above the moon have their full *eidetic* value. But what is brought about within the lunar sphere and below is always partial and imperfect, and sometimes even totally misshapen. Aristotle reasons quite intrepidly here. No deformity in life troubles him. In the first place, it is entirely natural insofar as it is material and accidental. And in the second place, it is possible only because an undistorted and absolutely perfect *eidos* lurks in its depths. If it weren't for the latter, we would not be able even to comprehend deformity precisely as deformity. Only in comparison with the eternal beauty of the *eidos* can the ugliness of the thing be judged specifically as ugliness.

But apart from this amazing fearlessness for the fate of the *eidos*, Aristotle feels quite calm and contented. A given deformity has come about in life, but as the misshapen thing ascends to its beautiful and eternal *eidos* all its deformity fades. This notion of the presence of chance in matter will come in very handy when we consider the ultimate foundations of Aristotle's philosophy, which we now see as tragic.

But one more important explanation is necessary at this point. The Greek word *tyche*, which in Aristotle must be understood as *chance*, also means *fate* in ancient Greek. But the purely philosophical orientation of Aristotle's arguments prevents us from translating the term as *fate*. After all, *chance* is also *fate* for Aristotle. But for the ancient Greeks *fate* was a purely mythological concept, not a philosophical one, whereas for Aristotle it was not mythological at all but purely philosophical. To put it bluntly, Aristotle absolutely did not want to reduce all of reality to fixed concepts and join them in a strictly logical and peremptory way.

We have already said that for Aristotle reality is endless motion or it is full of motion; and we shall speak of this again in a moment. But pure *eidos* is not some motion. It is the rational principle of motion and its meaningful shaping but is certainly not motion itself. The latter can be both invested with meaning and meaningless, i.e., both beautiful

151

and deformed. Consequently, for our judgments of reality fully to correspond to it, we must find in it not only a conceptual structure and not only its dead, immobile skeleton, however meaningful it may be. A realistic explanation of reality necessarily also requires the assumption of an extra-*eidetic* factor, in other words, a factor allowing for concepts to be realized not merely in a fixed and logically explainable way. After all, for all our logic we do not know what will happen tomorrow or the day after. Indeed we don't know even what will happen to us and everyone else, the whole surrounding world, an hour, a minute, or a second from now. Can we then, if we are to depict reality realistically, omit the category of chance, i.e., any kind of unexpectedness and suddenness, any kind of happenings devoid of any logical and *eidetic*, or structurally meaningful justification and explanation?

This is why Aristotle, reasoning in a manner that had absolutely nothing to do with any mythology, found it necessary for the sake of the most elementary realism to include in his description of reality the notion of matter understood as chance. And although he did not definitively deny mythology, in this case, we repeat, his conception of matter was totally unmythological and absolutely realistic. Chance was a purely philosophical concept for him here. On the basis of this philosophical concept he might, and in fact did, draw completely unphilosophical conclusions. But in his analysis of the four principles of the structure of what exists, he remained nothing but a philosopher. And if one wishes to translate the term he used not as *chance* but as *fate*, it still remained a purely philosophical notion for him; fate in this case was not an object of faith for him or some religious dogma or a remnant of a popular mythological tradition. *Chance* or *fate* were merely philosophical categories for him.

True, fate had been a philosophical category for Plato as well, and subsequently became one for the stoic philosophers. But only in Aristotle did this category achieve relentless precision. As far as contemporary thinkers are concerned, fate in this sense holds nothing mysterious for them. Dialectical materialism discusses the dialectics of necessity and chance, as well as universal causality and, on the other hand, freedom of the individual. Furthermore, one can say that without the principle of chance the category of matter itself would lose all meaning to us because for us, too, matter is not at all a fixed system of logically petrified concepts. **The only work in which Aristotle comes forth as a fundamental materialist, i.e., teaches that matter is the principle of the living reality of the world existing around us, is his theory of matter as the realm of chance** (however, the chance mobility of matter does not prevent, but on the contrary demands that he recognize the immobile and completely uncasual category of form — *eidos*).

Anticipating a little, we must also mention that if the *eidos* of a thing discloses the thing's meaningful essence, nothing prevents us from taking all these ideas of things together and getting what, as we shall see below, Aristotle calls Mind or Intellect, which is the Idea of Ideas for him, and hence supreme existence. But then the sixth-century AD writer Joannes Lydus, who sees in Aristotle the complete exclusion of all fate, is not far wrong. If everything is ruled by supreme reason, or Mind, then no place is left for any chance or, consequently, any fate. Aristotle himself says approximately the same thing in his *Magna Moralia* (II, 8). Indeed in his discussion of supreme reason, Aristotle speaks only of Mind as the prime mover but says nothing of fate. From our strictly historical point of view today, it is hardly admissible to avoid completely any category of fate in studying ancient pagan philosophy, including the philosophy of Aristotle, otherwise we would be dealing not with ancient or pagan but with purely European and even Christian philosophy. An element of fate, as we just saw, is undoubtedly present in Aristotle. But one can quite definitely note a certain monotheistic tendency, not yet very clear to Aristotle himself, in his discussion of Mind.

And so, no thing exists without matter since matter is the principle of its existence. And no thing exists without its *eidos* or form since the real form of a thing is precisely the thing itself: remove its form from a thing, and the thing will disintegrate, i.e., will be destroyed. Now let us ask ourselves whether these two principles are enough to define a thing, or whether some other principle must be advanced. It is immediately evident that however necessary these two principles may be, they are far from formulating the **motion** of the thing. For without motion one cannot imagine anything at all. But the form of a thing is not yet its motion, since a thing can also be without motion, at rest. Similarly, the matter of a thing is also not yet the thing itself, i.e., is not its motion, since we imagine matter primarily spatially. The form of a thing can be in motion, but conceived in itself it is not yet motion, just as the matter of a thing can be in motion but is not motion itself. **Motion is a quite specific category which cannot be reduced to any other.** It must be recognized as such, on a par with form and matter.

Aristotle waxes eloquent on the necessity and ineradicability of motion: "Now the existence of motion is asserted by all who have anything to say about nature, because they all concern themselves with the construction of the world and study the question of becoming and perishing, which processes could not come about without the existence of motion ... every one would admit that in each kind of motion it is that which is capable of that motion that is in motion: thus it is that which is capable of alteration that is altered and that which is capable of local change that is in locomotion: and so there must be something capable of being burned before there can be a process of being burned, and something capable of burning before there can be a process of burning" (*Physics* VIII, 1).

Thus, according to Aristotle, motion is as fundamental a category as matter and form. Moreover, two other circumstances come into play. First, there is an unlimited number of various types of motion; and second, if there is motion in nature and in the universe, motion at zero speed, i.e., rest, is also possible. The main point, however, is that Aristotle approaches the problem of motion not only as a natural scientist, but also as a philosopher. And the philosophical characterization of motion leads to issues which go far beyond the limits of a natural-scientific understanding of motion. Aristotle addresses the question of the very **possibility** of the category of motion. Plato had already dealt with this issue in his day. But we shall concentrate on how Aristotle tackles the problem of the origin of motion.

154

If a thing is moving, it means that another thing exists which set it in motion. But the same reasoning obviously applies to the motion of this second thing. Clearly this second thing moves because it was set in motion by some third thing, and so on. If we go off into an infinite regress to explain the motion of the first thing, will this be a true explanation, or, by referring ourselves to ever new things, will we not then be renouncing all explanation of our moving thing? To put an end to this infinite passing from one thing to another, Aristotle requires us to recognize that there exists such a thing whose motion no longer needs referral to some other thing. This thing moves of itself and to move does not require any other thing which would move it. In other words, if all things move, and if some definite cause must exist for motion, one must admit some autonomic motion, some cause which is **a cause for its own self.** This is *the third principle* of the existence of things, the third principle of being, which must be recognized on equal terms with the matter and the form or *eidos* of a thing. Of course in our daily experience, practically every thing acquires its motion from some other thing. But at the level of philosophical examination of motion, we must recognize, according to Aristotle, that in existence there is a self-propelled cause and that this self-motion is reflected in one way or another in the real dependence of the motion of one thing on the motion of another. This auto-motion, this spontaneity, is diffused throughout the whole universe, although everywhere it exists and is manifested in different ways.

Let us advance one more step, and Aristotle's four-principle formula of existence will be basically complete. A thing moves, and some cause exists for this motion. But specifically **where** is this thing moving, **in what direction** is it moving, and is motion possible at all without being directed? Clearly, every moving thing is necessarily characterized by some direction of its motion. This is obvious if only because every thing functions in some way, exists for some end and was created for some purpose. We shall not speak of the animate world and the motion of individual living creatures, which of course always has both a definite reason and a definite goal. But let us take an inanimate, inorganic thing, a stone, say, outside the window, or the water in the nearest stream. These things are certainly inorganic. But can one have some conception of them without a conception of an organism as a certain entity? For all these inorganic things also have their history and may have lost their former integrity or will acquire it. They may have once entered into the composition of live organisms or were such themselves, as, for example, fossilized mollusks or amber. In general, spontaneous motion and mechanically caused motion are two concepts which do not exist the one without the other, just as white does not exist without black, heavy without light, lofty without low and so on. Thus the concept of mechanical motion is unthinkable without the concept of spontaneous motion.

Thus, if one ascribes motion to things, and if a motion is impossible without a corresponding cause, and if every cause presupposes a cause-in-itself, or spontaneous motion, such an understanding of cause obviously has universal significance and no thing is conceivable without it.

Here the need arises for one more category without which the category of motion is unthinkable. For one cannot conceive of motion in the abstract, i.e., without the result it produces. We spoke of the directedness of every motion just now. This directedness testifies to the fact that there is a definite result at each point of the motion. If we do not perceive the result of the motion, then obviously we do not perceive the direction of this motion either. And if we do not perceive the results of the action of the cause, then we do not perceive the action itself of the cause. A cause and its result can of course be thought of separately. The lofty can also be thought of apart from the low, and in perceiving the color white it is not at all necessary instantly to imagine the color black. Yet all the same, the one is impossible without the other. And if the cause of a thing's motion led this thing somewhere, brought it to a certain state, furnished it with certain properties or qualities, then every cause in its actual functioning presupposes some **aim**. A house is built as a result of certain causes, whether they be the architect's plans or the efforts of the workers who brought the bricks and arranged them in a certain order. But the completed house is neither the plan of this house, nor its construction. We live not in the plan of the house, but in the house itself, not in the house's construction processes, but in the house itself. This means that the house is not only its own cause and is not a cause at all. It is its own aim. What exactly is an aim? One might say a lot on the subject, but one thing is clear, the aim of a thing is neither its form, nor its matter, nor its cause. The aim is a specific category which cannot be reduced to any other. *And this is Aristotle's fourth principle of the existence of any thing.*

*10. The doctrine of measure.* At this point we must at least briefly discuss a general aesthetic principle of antiquity, which, although Aristotle does not set it forth systematically in one place, can be systematically summarized under one heading once one has considered all Aristotle's views on the subject. It seems to us that if this topic is not presented too generally and dryly, the **category of measure** will prove a necessary consequence of Aristotle's theory of the four principles of life and being just discussed. It is easy to prove that for Aristotle measure is not simply a quantitative principle and not simply a qualitative principle, but first and foremost an **eidetic** principle, as well as a **causal-purposive** principle, to say nothing of its **materiality.**

For example, in the sphere of **ethics**, the best is a sort of mean between two opposites, i.e., a certain measure of moral orientation between the two. Thus courage is the middle point between fear and reckless bravery; generosity, between stinginess and prodigality; magnanimity, between self-conceit and self-abasement (*Nicomachean Ethics* II, 7; III, 4; IX, 5).

The same measure, for Aristotle, is also observed in the **aesthetic** sphere (*On Poetics* 7).

He sees the same phenomenon in the realm of **politics** as well: "To the size of states there is a limit, as there is to other things, plants, animals, implements; for none of these retain their natural power when they are too large or too small, but they either wholly lose their nature, or are spoiled. For example, a ship which is only a span long will not be a ship at all, nor a ship a quarter of a mile long; yet there may be a ship of a certain size, either too large or too small, which will still be a ship, but bad for sailing" (*Politics* VII, 4).

157

Finally, the category of measure plays a big role for Aristotle in astronomy as well. To understand the passage we shall quote below, one must bear in mind that the faster a body moves, the more space it covers in one and the same time interval, and that, consequently, a body moving infinitely fast at once occupies all the possible spaces for its passage, i.e., it is at rest. The sky, according to Aristotle, moves at this maximum speed, hence it is at rest.

When it is a question not of a heavenly body, but of any body which moves with a finite speed, the slower the body moves the less it is like the heavens. And yet there is some point of comparison to the heavens in every body moving with a finite speed, insofar as the measure of its motion is infinitely small. Now the following extract becomes clear: "If the motion of the heaven is the measure of all movements whatever in virtue of being alone continuous and regular and eternal, and if, in each kind, the measure is the minimum, and the minimum movement is the swiftest, then, clearly, the movement of the heaven must be the swiftest of all movements" (*On the Heavens* II, 4).

In other words, **Aristotle's doctrine of measure is the direct result of his theory of the four-principle structure of every thing.** Since the *eidos* of a thing is identified with its matter, this identity is the measure of the functioning of *eidos* and matter; and since cause is likewise identical with aim in the given thing, this identification must also be viewed as the measure of the functioning of these two categories. If only because the motion and aim of a thing enter into its very definition, measure in the thing's meaningful actualization must also enter into its definition.

*11. General formulation of the four-principle structure, and its aesthetic and creative foundation.* Up to now we have been expounding Aristotle's four principles more or less separately and independently, whereas for Aristotle himself they unquestionably represent something integral and indivisible. For Aristotle has a truly mosaic-like style of thinking. His concepts are extremely differentiated and minute. He likes to distinguish endlessly, to analyze infinite details and find new nuances where others think too generally. And he does so in discussing the four principles of an animate structure, which could of course be presented more as a whole, in a less minute and more general, much more intelligible form.

Let us formulate these four principles in a more general way, and then show how this single integral principle operates in various areas of existence without the minute compartmentalization which Aristotle imparts to his reasoning, or rather with the same minuteness but synthetically and more intelligibly.

And so, we are dealing with the definition of a thing. Specifically, a thing is (let us convey Aristotle's meaning more comprehensibly), first, **matter,** second, **form,** third, **operative cause,** and fourth, a **certain expediency.** *Eidos* (form) does not exist separately, but is always embodied in matter. And so we shall speak of materially realized form, a formulation which, it seems to us, will be understandable to everyone. The fact that every thing functions in some way — for example a tree grows, a stone changes its shape depending upon the surrounding environment — will hardly be questioned by anyone. For all things change: grow younger or older, acquire a purer form, decay or simply get destroyed and die. A cherry tree produces a certain type of fruit. And these cherries are the aim which the tree pursued while it was growing. A child's sled gradually gets rickety and finally breaks. And this breakage is the end at which the growing ricketiness of the sled inevitably aimed. Would not it be simpler to say that every thing has a causal-purposive aspect, that it occurred through some cause and reached some goal, positive or negative? Would not it be simpler to reduce Aristotle's complicated train of reasoning to a single universally intelligible phrase, namely, **each thing is a materialized form with a causal-purposive function?**

Similarly, the four-fold structure of a thing can be expressed simply without reference to any of Aristotle's four causes, in the form of a single principle, also intelligible to all but naturally requiring some explanation. What is this principle? After all, if we grasped it, the whole of Aristotle's highly complex philosophy would appear to us in a most simple and intelligible form, which there would be no need to explain. Of course we would have to put it "in our own words", as they say, but there's nothing at all wrong in that.

Let us take the correlation of *eidos* (form, idea) and matter. In everyday life matter is understood too prosaically, simply as a material out of which something is made. But even if one understands matter as simple material, the shaping of matter to get some kind of object from it already presupposes a certain, albeit primitive, **aesthetic and creative** principle giving shape to matter.

There was some wood lying in the yard, some boards or sticks and logs. But I summoned a carpenter and told him to make a good, sturdy, attractive kennel for my dog so it could take shelter there in rainy or frosty weather. The carpenter began to consult with me over what kind of sides to build for this doghouse, what kind of roof, and so on. I chatted with him for a long time. A certain type of wall didn't seem right to us, and we decided on another kind. We also decided on a particular form for the roof of the kennel. Learning my intentions, the carpenter said: "Wouldn't it be better, in the interest of clarity, first to sketch this kennel on paper?" And after I had drawn the plan of the kennel with the carpenter, he asked me a few more questions, because he didn't want the kennel to be drafty or water to penetrate it so the dog could comfortably escape bad weather, and he didn't want the opening to be too big or too small, etc. The carpenter then puttered around for quite some time with the planks, did much sawing and planing, much nailing and hammering. And the result was a fine kennel, cosy for the dog and agreeable to my eyes.

The question now is, where in this doghouse is its *eidos* (form, idea) and where is its matter? When I look at it, I quite forget to think of any *eidos* or any matter. For me it is simply a doghouse and nothing more. But it is not enough to say this. The thing is that both the carpenter and I pondered before building it. The *eidos* itself is nothing; at the most, it is the carpenter's and my thought, our sketch on paper. But the dog will live not in the idea of the kennel but in the kennel itself, not in the blueprint of the kennel but in the kennel itself. And my friends admire not the *eidos* of the kennel but the kennel itself, and not the wood that was lying around in my yard or garden and out of which the kennel was made, but the kennel itself.

In other words, the materialization of the *eidos* of the kennel in its matter is none other than a successfully and expediently executed product, i.e., the result of work bearing a direct relation to the skill, and therefore ultimately to the artistic aspiration of the craftsman himself. Of course a doghouse is a very elementary example, where creativity manifests itself minimally, although the carpenter can make the kennel well or badly, make it beautiful or ugly. But even works of art can be both good and bad. In fact, the principle of form's embodiment in matter, of which we spoke above, is always necessarily only a certain creative principle, either good or bad. In daily life, too, we speak of the form given to some material. But our recognition of this form is always too prosaic. We know neither what the *eidos* of the thing is — at the most, to us it is only its plan; nor what the matter of the thing is — at the most, it is only its raw material. But Aristotle has analyzed the concept of the *eidos* of the thing in the most refined way; and so subtly and elegantly has he elaborated this category that whole dissertations and thick tomes are written on how he understands matter. In this work it will be sufficient to point out only the indispensable general **creative principle** underlying the correlation of *eidos* (or form) and matter in Aristotle. In any case our focus corresponds to Aristotle's central position on this question.

Aristotle has just as painstakingly elaborated the two other principles of a thing's structure, namely the principle of the operative cause, as a result of which the thing came into being, and the principle of its end shape, by which it differs from other things made of the same materials. Say we are looking at a painting on which is depicted a sinking ship, or a peaceful landscape, or a bouquet of flowers, or a person's portrait. The artist worked hard to give his painting the appearance it has. He tried out various colors, many times erased some detail or other. Moreover, he studied for many years in order to become a mature artist. He received an education, had certain ideas, defended them or argued against other ideas. But do we see all these operative causes in the painting? No, we do not at all. Of course there is a whole scholarly discipline, namely art criticism, which teaches us to identify and study all the details and the origin of a given painting. But can one say that paintings are created only for professors of art history? No. Although paintings can be endlessly analyzed, they are created for absolutely everybody and are perceived by everyone quite spontaneously, without any analysis, without any scholarly details. Only afterwards, after the painting has been perceived as a certain indivisible whole, can one, and sometimes one even should (although one may not always succeed), analyze the painting, study its minutest details and discuss the reasons for its creation. The same thing must be said of the aim which this painting achieves, its results as a certain whole and its effect on those looking at it. If one looks at a painting spontaneously, one sees neither its causes nor its aims but only the picture itself. And again this is true not only of works of art. For even all those things which we are not at all inclined to treat aesthetically have also come from somewhere and pursue a certain end; furthermore, it makes no difference whether all these causes and all these results of the state of the thing at a given moment are good or bad. Thus the operative cause and the end result of a thing are also distinguishable only in our mind. By themselves they do not differ in the slightest. And I sit down not on the cause of the chair, but the chair itself, not on the end result of the chair's provenance but on the chair itself.

Therefore, to sum up what we have just said: **Aristotle based his theory of the four-principle structure of things exclusively on the premise that every thing is the result of creative activity.** Moreover, it is unimportant whether the creative product is good or bad. Note, too, that in constructing his theory of the causal and purposive principles, Aristotle had a definite intention in mind. Actually the first pair of his four principles, namely *eidos* and matter, express Aristotle's aesthetic and creative approach to reality quite fully. But if we sit down not on the idea of the chair but on the chair itself, and not on the matter of the chair but on the chair itself, and hence conclude that every chair as the material realization of an *eidos* is the product of a certain creative activity, or a work of art (whether good or bad), one could just as well say that we sit down not on the principle of the chair's aesthetic reproduction but simply on the chair, and therefore the aestheticity of the chair is also a rather abstract category. It is this abstraction in his construct of the thing that Aristotle obliterates by bringing the origin and the end result of the thing into its construction. The introduction of the latter two principles makes the thing both actually operative and expediently directed. **In other words, the latter two principles transform the thing into the process of life, make it a living organism, as a result of which the aestheticity of the thing is utterly identical to its material perfection.** Therefore a beautiful dish which we use for food proves to be both very beautiful and very sturdy; and a beautiful hat which we wear becomes both a piece of creative craftsmanship and a durable headpiece made of good quality material, comfortable to wear, and generally equipped with all the features of optimum and quite practical usefulness.

In this way, these two principles alone, cause and aim, make a beautiful thing not only an aesthetic object but also one meeting all the requirements of the most ordinary use. In other words, for Aristotle as for Chernyshevsky later on, "the beautiful is life"; "Beautiful is the being in which we see life as it should be according to our notions; beautiful is the object which manifests life or brings life to mind."[1] Naturally the agreement of these two thinkers on this one point does not in the least prevent them from differing radically on many other philosophical and aesthetic questions.

It is important to note that the four principles Aristotle speaks of can be embodied in a thing in the most perfect way, in which case they create an organism that is constructed not only expediently, but well and even beautifully, too. Thus the existence of a work of art depends upon the degree of perfection in the integral unity of the four principles. If the degree of their embodiment is lacking in measure, is insufficient or on the contrary excessive, the organism will be characterized by defectiveness, consequently it will lack aestheticity, beauty, usefulness, expediency, and will be an example of something bad, unsuccessfully executed, ugly and inexpedient. **All the diversity of the material world is based on varying correlations of** *eidos* **(form, idea) and matter in their causal-purposive**

**embodiment.** This is why the four principles can be present in both the most beautiful and the most hideous thing. Both have their own measure of correlation, different each time, otherwise the world would present a boring monotone of identically constructed objects.

*12. The aesthetic and creative principle in connection with Aristotle's theory of the ascending levels, or hierarchical structure, of life and being.* Now all we have left to do is examine how Aristotle applies this primary aesthetic and creative principle to various stages of development of life and being. The fact is that the basic aesthetic principle we formulated above is applied by Aristotle in very different ways because for him, as for all of ancient philosophy, there was no indifferent being lacking all value. To the natural scientist of the Modern Era, all objects under study have the same value: in a biological sense a frog is in no way less valuable than the most beautiful, developed and intelligent living being. The moon is no worse than the sun to us, and our sun is no better or worse than any other heavenly body. Therefore there is no top or bottom in nature from the point of view of value. Everything can equally be considered both top and bottom, highest and lowest, depending only on the point of departure we have chosen to start with; and there is an infinite number of such reference points. We find a completely different conception of life and being in the ancient philosophers. For them some things are more valuable, others less; or to use the terms from Aristotle we have accepted, some are more aesthetic, others less.

It is interesting that the ancient thinkers, elemental materialists though they were, established corresponding temporal and spatial locations for objects of differing values. What was fine and valuable was higher spatially and more comprehensive and richer temporally. For the ancients the highest level of spatial existence and most all-embracing position in time was realized in the sky, which to them was not simply empty space going off into the infinite distance but a quite definite sphere of life and being at a definite distance from the earth. This distance was known because, according to the poet Hesiod, Hephaestus thrown out of heaven tumbled nine days to the earth. By

164

using the precise data provided in such myths, contemporary physicists could easily calculate the distance from the sky to the earth with utmost accuracy.

In a certain sense of the word, the sky is even some kind of firmly established cupola. It is no accident that ancient poets speak of the iron or copper sky, just as old Russian had a word equivalent to the firmament to indicate not so much physical solidity and firmness as the spiritual affirmation of the heavenly cupola. The gods, whom the ancients conceived as certain principles of truth, beauty and all existence in general, mainly lived in the sky. And if they were also called the Olympian gods it was because the famous Mount Olympus in Greece was considered to be so high and so sacred that its summit was thought to touch the sky itself or be identical to it.

It is quite clear that with such a view of the qualitatively diverse, hierarchical shaping of life, it was to receive a quite varied aesthetic shaping as well.

Aristotle's basic aesthetic principle, as is the case with almost all the ancient philosophers, changes almost unrecognizably depending upon its sphere of application. Let us touch on these levels of existence, beginning with the lowest forms and gradually moving up to the highest.

*a) The aesthetic role of matter.* It is clear that matter is lowest of all for Aristotle. But even here his basic aesthetic principle compelled Aristotle to see in matter not simply some shapeless mass of dead materials. Matter bears with it the very same four-principle structure of existence we spoke of earlier. But naturally it bears it in a very specific way. To be sure, matter is defined by Aristotle as deprivation of all forms. But this is not simply the absence of all forms, but is an infinite creative possibility as well. Matter is the principle of the actualization of *eidos*, or form. But without this actualization of the idea-forms, it is evident that they would not exist at all. Later we shall see that even the highest, supreme levels of cosmic development have their specific matter. The gods, in the eyes of the ancients, were also material bodies; only one must keep in mind that this matter was very fine and all-pervasive, i.e., they were ethereal bodies.

165

*b) Nature as a work of art.* Matter manifests itself first and foremost in various spatial and temporal forms. Unfortunately we cannot study this question in all its depth here. But one thing is certain: neither time nor space are indifferent, infinite black holes for Aristotle, but always have their physiognomy, always seethe with vital strivings and always have some value.

Of great importance is Aristotle's theory of nature. Here, too, he remained a true ancient, for whom nature was always full of countless possibilities. For if the basic principle established by Aristotle is applied to nature, natural things and all of nature taken in its entirety are necessarily endowed with some meaning. As the unity of matter and form, nature to Aristotle is full of all kinds of causes and all kinds of aims.

Many scholars have unduly exaggerated the significance of the purposive principle necessary in Aristotle's view of nature, and have reduced all of his philosophy of nature to a teleology, or philosophy of ends. This interpretation is quite incorrect, because, apart from aims, causes, ideas, and above all matter itself, are active in Aristotle's nature. Therefore it is much closer to the truth to speak not of Aristotle's teleology but of his aesthetic philosophy of nature, i.e., his vision of nature as an integral organism creatively constructed according to his four principles. It goes without saying that as a result, the entire cosmos is aesthetically shaped for Aristotle.

Let us now ascend one step higher in the hierarchy of existence.

*c) The soul is nothing other than the principle of a living body.* After inorganic and organic nature we pass on to the realm of animate beings, including the whole human world. Here, too, Aristotle's four principles of structure are in the foreground. What is specific to this level is the sphere of the soul, which is also understood quite diversely, from the propagation and growth of living beings to the presence in them of a highly developed psychology. Let us not be surprised that Aristotle views the soul as an organizing, directing and even commanding principle. For the soul is also a sort of *eidos*. Only it is not *eidos* in general, but "a substance in the sense of the form [*eidos*] of a natural body having life potential within it" (*On the Soul* II, 1). In other words, according to Aristotle, the soul is simply the life of the body, only understood in a particular sense. Aristotle's analytical and more minutely articulated manner of expression leads him to speak not merely of life, but of "life potentials", and not merely of "life potentials", but of the "physical possibilities" of life as well. This is why for Aristotle, as for many ancient philosophers, the soul governs the body. If one does not take this notion too literally and too absolutely, since often it is not the soul that governs the body but the body the soul, but if one understands it *eidetically*, in the sense, for instance, that the multiplication table "governs" all our quantitative computations, then Aristotle's definition of the soul is quite comprehensible. The soul's governance of the body is not logical or mechanical or ethical but vitally creative or, we would say, aesthetic. According to how the body of an animal behaves, we can determine the essence of this animal. In observing a human body we observe its inner causal-purposive directedness in giving meaning to the vital element in one way or another. This means that for Aristotle the soul is primarily the principle of a living body's aesthetic shaping.

Generally speaking, Aristotle distinguishes three types of soul: vegetal, sensitive (animal) and rational. Aristotle examines the four principles of aesthetic shaping at each of these levels and ascribes a specific character to them in each case. A rational soul also has its *eidos* and its matter and its causal-purposive directedness. In this respect it is entirely analogous to living nature. The only difference is that in nature the creative and created elements are one and the same, whereas in man the creating subject differs from the work of art he creates. Hence those who foreground the merely imitative character of art in Aristotle have an incorrect understanding of him.

These scholars say that for Aristotle art is the imitation of nature. Abstractly speaking this statement makes some sense. But in actuality nature for Aristotle is already a work of art in itself insofar as *eidos* and matter, i.e., the inner and outer, are fused into one indivisible whole in it. Therefore, from Aristotle's point of view, one could say that nature, too, is an imitation of art. True, there is some inconvenience in expressing his position in this manner because the modern reader associates such a thesis with various purely subjectivist theories. Therefore we shall say that for Aristotle art is the imitation of nature, while keeping in mind the important elaboration of his position we just formulated.

Thus, in our ascent of the steps of existence we have reached the rational soul, and are now faced with two fundamental aspects of Aristotle's philosophy. We shall briefly touch on these two issues, which are in fact the capstone of Aristotle's philosophy taken as a whole.

### 13. The aesthetic and creative principle in its culmination.

*a) Every material body is something, i.e., has a certain* eidos, *or meaning. The* eidos *of a living body is its life principle, i.e., its soul. But any soul moving a body also has its own* eidos, *which Aristotle calls Mind. And so the soul, according to Aristotle, is nothing but the energy or actuality of Mind or thought. But "the actuality of thought is life"* (Metaphysics *XII, 7), hence all that lives is animate, i.e., has its own* eidos.

Thus, every soul, every type of soul as a result of its four-principle structure is first and foremost an *eidos*. But a human soul actually existing in life is, according to Aristotle, a mixture of various souls, mainly a vegetal, sensitive and rational soul. The value of these souls differs greatly. The vegetal and animal aspects of the soul are eternally in a process of becoming. This means that vegetal life can originate, bloom, wither and, most importantly, die. Therefore from Aristotle's point of view it would be very difficult to speak of the immortality of an individual human soul. Its vegetal and animal aspects can reach completion and end, and thus does an individual human soul die, too.

But here is the hitch. Every soul is first and foremost an *eidos*, actualized or shaped in a certain way. But the *eidos* itself, however we approach it, is as unsusceptible to change, including death, as the multiplication table, which does not admit of spatial and temporal categories. It would make no sense to say that a one or a two or a three, etc., have some odor, are somehow tangible to our fingers

168

or our body in general, are in some way visible or audible. In other words, the individual human soul is certainly mortal, but its *eidos* can in no respect be considered mortal because it is quite impossible and senseless to apply the category of time to it.

Here one must also keep in mind that the ideas, whatever they be, do not exist in isolation, because this would mean they were distributed in space at certain intervals from each other. But neither the concept of space nor that of time applies to the ideas. Consequently, all possible ideas exist together and indivisibly, as an integral whole. And in this sense all the ideas taken as a whole represent what Aristotle calls Mind. As for a rational soul, it is nothing else but a "place for ideas". This *eidetic* mind in a person is seen by Aristotle as something liable to no spatial or temporal categories. This is what is immortal. The transition from the concept of soul to the concept of mind is the first of the culmination points of Aristotle's philosophy as a whole.

*b) Mind is the Idea of all Ideas.* Thus, in existence there is nothing higher than the ideas, or than Mind. Aristotle spent much effort proving the paramount importance of the concept of Mind. As the loftiest sphere of existence as a whole, Mind is, to put it concisely, the supreme concept for Aristotle. It is the idea of ideas. In the human soul the rational *eidos*, being tied to other types of *eidos*, is relative and only potential, insofar as it is limited by various other less perfect kinds of souls. But taken in itself, Mind is bound by nothing and depends only upon itself. In this sense it is eternally immobile. Furthermore, whereas the individual human soul moves here and there in different directions, the Mind of the whole cosmos, which comprehends absolutely everything, cannot itself move since it has already embraced everything, and therefore nothing exists to or into which it could move.

*c) Despite its utter voidness of sensible matter, Mind contains its own purely mental matter without which it would not be a work of art.* No philosophers before Aristotle admitted the existence of matter in Mind. And if they did, it was as a result of a still incomplete differentiation of the concept of Mind or *eidos*. But nobody had so acutely and fundamentally contrasted matter and Mind as Aristotle did. And now it turns out that matter, so essentially different from Mind, finds an absolute place for itself in Mind itself. However, this matter is not the sensible matter which is the object of our physical sensations. It is mental or intellectual matter, matter endowed with meaning, differing in nothing from *eidos*, intra-*eidetic* matter. We must fully account for why Aristotle found it necessary to thrust matter into the heart of Mind itself. The reason will completely escape those who do not grasp the universality of Aristotle's four principles of structure. In accordance with this construct, matter is necessary to give form to *eidos*. Without it, the idea would remain only an abstract possibility, *eidos* for Aristotle being only one element in every thing, insofar as every thing is a work of art. Without its mental matter, Mind, according to Aristotle, would not find its actualization, would not have its beautiful form, and consequently would not be a work of art.

After all, everyone realizes that to produce a work of art one must first have this or that physical material, in itself not yet bearing a direct relation to art. A sculptor comes, starts to work on the shapeless blocks of marble, and a beautiful statue appears. His artistic intuition made Aristotle introduce a certain type of matter into the heart of Mind itself, absolute, cosmic, divine as it may be.

*d) Other properties of absolute Mind following from Aristotle's general four-principle structure of all that exists: immobile prime mover, absolute regularity of existence, "thinking on thinking", coincidence of subject and object in one indivisible point, absolute supra- and intra-cosmicity.* Finally, the four-principle formula of life and being contains, as we know, the aspects of cause and aim. Applied to Aristotle's Mind, these concepts lead to his splendid theory of Mind as prime mover and absolute expediency. But one must not, as is often done, separate the four fundamental principles too much. Naturally, each one of them is something particular and specific, and each deserves special attention. But, as we have already said several times, these four principles are absolutely indivisible in their existence. Therefore one cannot too literally separate the Mind of

170

the cosmos from the cosmos itself, just as any *eidos* of a thing cannot be detached from the thing itself. The cosmic Mind, or *eidos* of the cosmos, is at the same time identical to the cosmos. And if the cosmos moves, then in that sense the cosmic Mind also moves or, more exactly, is the cause of all motion, is the aim of all motion. The identity of *eidos* and matter, as we said above, is the reason that a thing is an organism, hence the entire cosmos is a beautiful, eternally living organism. But the cosmos is the only possible form of existence and the only possible universal object of thinking. Consequently the Mind of the cosmos is also the sole and absolute mind comprehending itself, since it has absorbed everything. It is thinking on thinking, its thinking is its activity, and its inherent activity is thinking. In other words, the subject and object of thinking coincide in a single indivisible point, just as, generally speaking, the four fundamental elements of the four-principle structure of all that exists also coincide in this thinking as in a single point.

*14. Aristotle's three concepts of Mind as prime mover.* Contemporary scholars have advanced the notion that Aristotle did not come up with a single concept of Mind, but that three such concepts can be found in his works. Since none of them are of secondary or incidental importance, but must be treated as three completely different approaches to the problem, we shall briefly touch on them all.

His **first** concept is still purely Platonic. Basically, it regards Mind as supreme and final Being upon which everything depends, including the World Soul, which is the principle of the entire cosmos' motion in a circle. Mind is nothing other than the realm of the gods, that is, of the ideas — the higher, supracosmic ones, and the lower, stellar ones.

The new and original element we find in Aristotle here as compared to Plato is his highly differentiated notion of Mind, which led him to his **second** concept.

In the first place, Mind for Aristotle is thinking and, in the second place, comprehending its own self, i.e., thinking on thinking. In the third place, Mind contains its own mental matter, which gives it the possibility of being eternal beauty (insofar as beauty is the ideal coincidence of idea and matter). In the fourth place, Mind is the idea of

171

ideas, and therefore shares the fate of any *eidos*, namely to be simultaneously distinct from matter (i.e., from the cosmos) and identical to it (i.e., to the cosmos).

In the fifth place, Aristotle is so enamored of everything intellectual, and consequently of Mind, that the World Soul loses its Platonic meaning for him. In a person only the rational soul is immortal, in contrast to the corporeal soul, which is entirely mortal. According to Aristotle, the soul of the world would have a humiliating existence, since it would be ordering the body of the cosmos to move not as is proper to it according to its nature, but according to its own arbitrary will; and since the body is completely different from the soul, the harmony of the world and its soul would be only accidental, so that the soul would be deprived of all bliss and would eternally abide in vain efforts and torments, like the mythical Ixion in the underworld, who for his sins was compelled to revolve eternally with a wheel of fire to which he was bound (*On the Heavens* II, 1).

From this last consideration follows Aristotle's **third** concept of Mind, considerably different from Plato's. The fact is that everything in the cosmos moves, and every movement depends on another movement; but this means that there is some motion which moves itself, and thus everything else as well. For Plato the World Soul governs the cosmos. For Aristotle, it is Mind which moves absolutely everything and consequently is life as eternal energy, but which is itself immobile, because its mobility would require some other cause, and there is nothing above it.

But not only this theory of the eternally motive and motionless Mind is interesting in Aristotle. It turns out that (since it is immobile), Mind itself aspires to nothing and, specifically, loves nothing. But everything else that exists besides Mind is eternally in motion, eternally aspires specifically to Mind as the supreme good, and eternally loves it. Mind loves nobody and nothing. But everything outside Mind loves mental life, because without it there would be no expediency and regularity anywhere.

Two comments must be made concerning this third, purely Aristotelian theory of Mind. First, if Mind, according to Aristotle, is the universal aim and therefore everything loves it, it is not correct that Mind, as the aim, does

172

not love anything, but (insofar as everything in general loves it) it must unquestionably love itself. For it differs from everything else only in that it is not a gradual attainment of the goal, but the aim already achieved. This means that it must love itself and nothing else, insofar as everything else is only aspiring to an end, and therefore imperfect. Aristotle, it is true, does not directly speak of Mind's love of itself, but he speaks of the eternal self-contentment of Mind and its resulting eternal bliss (*Metaphysics* XII, 7).

Second, this theory of Mind's love for itself and absence of love for everything else is a **characteristic ancient teaching**. As in everything else, Aristotle is a typical ancient thinker here. For Mind to him is not somebody, but only something. Or, to be more precise, Mind to Aristotle is not a personality, and only a person can love or hate. But why, one may ask, is Aristotle's Mind not personalized? After all, it is the Idea of Ideas, and maximally generalized, Plato's and Aristotle's Ideas are none other than gods. But the pagan gods were not personalized. The truth lies in the trivial thought that the gods were the result of the deification of the forces of nature (and, we would add, the material forces of society). So, there was no question of personalization here at all. All the personal traits ascribed to the mythological gods are ordinary everyday human qualities. Besides, man himself, according to Aristotle, is not a personality either but only reason. All the rest in him is the same as in animals. True, such a concept of the pagan gods makes them seem too rational, cold and remote from the concrete life of the human soul. But that is the way it is. With any other interpretation we lapse into a modernization of paganism and christianize what has no relation to Christianity.

*15. The nature of Aristotle's religiosity.* It is clear we have now reached an issue which cannot be formulated otherwise than the question of Aristotle's religion.

*a) Aristotle was infinitely far removed from the childish naivete of his people's religious and mythological concepts.* One need read only a few pages where Aristotle explains what he calls his "first philosophy" to be convinced of the complete originality of his philosophical thinking and its

173

utter independence of any dogmas of faith. He subjects to analysis the most ultimate, supreme and basic foundations of life. He is entirely fearless in so doing. Here, too, only what has been made intelligible, proved and brought into a system exists for him. In his philosophy there are simply no unproved and at the same time absolutely imperative dogmas of faith. Aristotle's philosophy is the domain of the all-conquering power of human reason. He never tires of extolling and glorifying reason, hence it is not surprising that he sees all of life as the realm of reason, culminating in the all-conquering power of Mind. Either Mind must be acknowledged as a reference-point in the chaos of life, in which case it is absolute truth and absolute necessity, although it is reached only gradually and as a result of endless and quite concrete mental efforts. Or, if Mind is not the basic principle, everything perishes in the sheer chaos of existence, unknowable in any respect. Aristotle was an apostle of reason, although he well understood that much knowledge causes many cares, or as he put it, "great learning gives many starting points" (fragment 62).[2]

*b) Aristotle's view of reason is not at all narrowly one-sided.* Of course, reason for Aristotle is not only the highest aspect of the soul, but the highest aspect of all of reality, the ultimate degree of its expediency and the system of its regularity. But he well knew that the actual human soul is not only full of rational aspirations. And what is more, some of its irrational faculties are useful and absolutely necessary as well. While we say that Aristotle loves rationalist constructions, we affirm at the same time that he loves life as well, and his rationalistic constructs are inseparable from his vital, passionate love for life. Generally speaking, this is a very broad topic.

One could cite a lot of examples to characterize Aristotle's personality in this respect. But we shall confine ourselves here to his discussion of the usefulness of anger and its necessity in various circumstances.

According to Seneca, "'Anger,' says Aristotle, 'is necessary, and no battle can be won without it — unless it fills the mind and fires the soul; it must serve, however, not as a leader, but as the common soldier'"; and "Aristotle

174

stands forth as the defender of anger, and forbids us to cut it out; it is, he claims, a spur to virtue."[3]

Cicero provides further testimony on the subject: "Again, what of the contention of the same Peripatetics that these selfsame disorders which we think need extirpating are not only natural but also bestowed on us by nature for a useful end? ... but that there is no substance in the petty logic of those who coldly argue like this: 'It is *right* to fight this battle; it is *proper* to contend for laws, for liberty, for country'; that these words have no meaning unless bravery breaks out in a blaze of anger. And they do not argue about warriors only; no stern commands in time of need are given, they think, without something of the keen edge of irascibility. Finally they do not approve of an orator unless he uses the prickles of irascibility, not merely in bringing an accusation but even in conducting a defence, and though the anger be not genuine, yet it should, they think, be feigned in language and gesture, that the delivery of the orator may kindle the anger of the hearer. In fine they say that they do not regard anyone, who does not know how to be angry, as a man, and to what we call mildness, they apply the term indifference with a bad meaning" ("Tusculan Disputations" IV, 19, *Cicero in 28 Volumes*, 18: 373-75).

Another passage with a less positive appraisal of anger says that just as smoke stings the eyes and prevents one from seeing what has been put into a drink, anger risen into consciousness dims it and prevents one from noticing the absurd errors of reason (fragment 660).

Thus, in his view of reason Aristotle always showed himself to be a realistically-minded philosopher. He was enamored of reason, but he also took account of the other aspects of the human soul.

*c) Aristotle always remained a son of his people and unmitigated patriot. To him the ancient beliefs of the Greek people were part of his heritage, wise and irrefutable.*

Aristotle lived in an environment of traditions connected with the cult of Asclepius, and even thought himself to be his distant descendant. It would seem impossible to combine strict philosophy and mythology. But for Aristotle philosophy, like any knowledge, arises from wonder at life's enigmas, and myths are also the result of astonishment at life, and manifest a certain wisdom. "A man who is puzzled and wonders thinks himself ignorant (whence even the lover of myth is in a sense a lover of Wisdom, for the myth is composed of wonders)" (*Metaphysics* I, 2).

Aristotle does not see myths as the delusions of ignorant people. In their own language they speak as it were of important problems, for instance the first substances or ideas, and are even practically useful: "Our forefathers in the most remote ages have handed down to their posterity a tradition, in the form of a myth, that these bodies are gods, and that the divine encloses the whole of nature. The rest of the tradition has been added later in mythical form with a view to the persuasion of the multitude and to its legal and utilitarian expediency; they say these gods are in the form of men or like some of the other animals, and they say other things consequent on and similar to these which we have mentioned. But if one were to separate the first point from these additions and take it alone — that they thought the first substances to be gods, one must regard this as an inspired utterance, and reflect that, while probably each art and each science has often been developed as far as possible and has again perished, these opinions, with others, have been preserved until the present like relics of the ancient treasure. Only thus far, then, is the opinion of our ancestors and of our earliest predecessors clear to us" (ibid., XII, 8).

Thus, Aristotle makes no use of myths in his own philosophy based on pure reason; but he respects the ancient myths of his people, seeing them as the result of collective popular wisdom.

*d) Grounding himself in sense experience and at the same time finding rational foundations in it, Aristotle constructs a foundation for the entire cosmos with the help of categories which must be seen as religious, so that his purely intellectual construct of the cosmos culminates in the doctrine of absolute universal regularity, or Mind.* One may wonder what is divine about recognizing the eternal regularity of the cosmos; it is only a question of the laws of nature and society, and there is nothing divine in them. But one cannot detach Aristotle from his times.

According to Aristotle, in the depths of being understood as absolute truth, nothing exists apart from this self-sufficient and autonomous eternal regularity of existence. Moreover, he arrived at all his cosmic constructions through science, logical arguments, and quite evident and independent human emotional experience. He is far from being always inclined to speak of gods. He easily denies the existence of the mythological poet Orpheus and attributes his songs to some actual person (fragment 7, as reported in Cicero, "De Natura Deorum" I, 38, *Cicero in 28 Volumes*, 19: 105). And he is just as ready to refer to the supracosmic Mind as a certain god. But the important thing is that religion and mythology add nothing new and unexpected to Aristotle, since all that was new and unexpected in his thinking he drew from scientific probing.

Philosophy proves to be independent of religious dogmas. Of itself it arrives at all-embracing existential conclusions, which could lead to religious analogies, not only in antiquity, but in the Middle Ages as well, when Aristotle's legacy, and particularly his theory of Mind as the prime mover governing the world, was interpreted in a Christian spirit.

A god is thought to be eternal, and Aristotle's cosmos is also eternal; a god is thought to be uncreated, and Aristotle's cosmos is also created by nobody and nothing. A god is thought to be almighty and always in action, and Aristotle's cosmos is also all-powerful and its action continuous and unending. God is completely self-moved and his motion depends on nothing except himself; Aristotle's matter is also automotive, and so is the cosmos arising out of it.

The self-sufficient regularity of the cosmos is contained within it. Hence it must be dependent upon nothing and absolutely free, comprehending only itself (and nothing else, for it has already enveloped everything else), and hence self-satisfied and utterly blissful. In his *Metaphysics* Aristotle writes: "And thinking in itself deals with that which is best in itself, and that which is thinking in the fullest sense with that which is best in the fullest sense. And thought thinks on itself because it shares the nature of the object of thought; for it becomes an object of thought in coming into contact with and thinking its objects, so that thought and object of thought are the same. For that which is *capable* of receiving the object of thought, i.e. the essence, is thought. But it is *active* when it *possesses* this object. Therefore the possession rather than the receptivity is the divine element which thought seems to contain, and the act of contemplation is what is most pleasant and best. If, then, God is always in that good state in which we sometimes are, this compels our wonder; and if in a better this compels it yet more. And God *is* in a better state. And life also belongs to God; for the actuality of thought is life, and God is that actuality; and God's self-dependent actuality is life most good and eternal" (*Metaphysics* XII, 7).

*e) Aristotle's philosophical daring.* Aristotle's pronouncements on Mind as prime mover and on the soul sometimes give an initial impression of some confession of faith. But our preceding account has indisputably shown that Aristotle reached conclusions having the form of theological tenets in the course of **scientific philosophical investigation**. What could have been simpler than to have made use of the traditional beliefs of his own people? But Aristotle did nothing of the sort. He reasoned and conducted his scholarly philosophical investigations in such a way that he absolutely did not need **any mythology**. And if his theory could then be interpreted mythologically, that had nothing to do with him. Although he loved the Greek myths and understood them profoundly, Aristotle did not use them anywhere in his scholarship.

It thus becomes clear why Aristotle was accused of impiety at the end of his life and a trial instituted against him. From the point of view of the people of his time the charge is quite understandable. He was religious and at the same time did not need any religion. People wanted to try him just as Socrates had been tried a few decades earlier. Socrates, too, had been religious. Nevertheless his very acute mind and his critically oriented philosophy had disturbed many people. And the Athenians decided it would be better if Socrates with his too critical mind were no longer, than for the old faith and piety to be shaken. But Aristotle, like Socrates, was quite fearless in this respect. The critical minds of Socrates and Aristotle were not afraid of shaking ancient beliefs, even though subjectively, internally, these beliefs were very dear to them. And the religious and philosophical fearlessness of both thinkers won out. Both remained faithful to old traditions, but their faith was not a slavish but a completely free one. Therefore the question of Aristotle's religiosity is a very complex one; and we suggest seriously pondering over what we have just said.

Another important point is that Aristotle's religious and philosophical fearlessness is quite characteristic of late classical antiquity with its very mature philosophical procedures. Let us add that in the thirteenth century at the waning of the Middle Ages, John Duns Scotus also claimed that without any higher revelation philosophy could formulate all the dogmas of faith which had previously been considered attainable only through divine revelation. This only proves that both Aristotle at the time of Greek classicism (fourth century BC) and John Duns Scotus at the time of medieval orthodoxy (thirteenth century AD) had both reached the most mature state of philosophy possible in their great eras. Both philosophers had attained the utmost limit of philosophical development in their culture, where separate truths were not simply founded one upon the other, but all went back to one supreme truth explaining both its own self and all of existence, and where the religious animation of being was seen not as a blind psychological process but a logical structure ascending to infinity, just as any series of finite natural numbers also stretches into infinity and also terminates in an infinitely remote point, above which there is nothing else and which contains supreme perfection. According to Aristotle in fragment 14, if we reverentially enter a temple, we should with all the greater reverence set about studying the cosmos, which Aristotle saw as the starry heavens.

In antiquity aesthetics did not exist as a special discipline, and Aristotle was not at all an aesthetician in this sense, yet we must recognize that his basic principle of life was a purely aesthetic one. In the same way, Aristotle was not a theologian or a theoretician of myth, but only a philosopher and theoretician of pure reason based on sense experience; and yet in investigating the utmost degree of truth seen to comprehend all the regularity and expediency of the cosmos, he arrived at his theory of a Mind possessing all the attributes of a divinity, so that a late commentator of Aristotle ascribes to him a doctrine of God as Mind or something beyond Mind (fragment 49). And Aristotle himself speaks without theologizing of the gods and their contemplation when he is talking of the best state of life; in illustration one could cite passages from his treatise "On the Virtues and Vices" (ch. 5) or fragments 10-11. On the other hand, he says nothing of the gods in his treatise *On the Heavens*. But when he is describing the absolute lightness of the sky and its so great stability that it would be degrading even for the soul of the cosmos to somehow affect the eternal and absolutely natural motion of the sky, he comes to the conclusion that such a view of the sky fully corresponds to what he calls *mantis*, or the prophetic (mantic) vision of the essence of things, as we might translate this Greek term.

Thus Aristotle is religious, but for him God is the Mind governing the cosmos. Hence he requires no religion in building the system of his philosophy.

*16. Complete unity of reason and life.* Now we can try to summarize Aristotle's philosophy as a whole, since we have already formulated its basic principles.

One cannot help being amazed at the originality of Aristotle's philosophy, the dialectical unity of concepts which other philosophers usually present too disjunctly.

To start with matter, for example, there is no such matter for Aristotle that is just a shapeless heap of who-knows-what. It is penetrated through and through with life and reason, so that it is even difficult to separate life and meaning in Aristotle. He endlessly scrutinizes this matter bursting with life, and is endlessly happy to discover in it the minutest details in their vital interrelation. Aristotle wrote whole treatises devoted to the anatomy and physiology of the animal world, for example, in which with childlike ingenuousness and delighted surprise he tries to detect and formulate countless details of the life process.

To give a notion of Aristotle's practical wisdom, we shall quote the profound observations on people at different ages found in his *Rhetoric*. Here is what we read about youth: "To begin with the Youthful type of character.

Young men have strong passions, and tend to gratify them indiscriminately. Of the bodily desires, it is the sexual by which they are most swayed and in which they show absence of self-control. They are changeable and fickle in their desires, which are violent while they last, but quickly over: their impulses are keen but not deep-rooted, and are like sick people's attacks of hunger and thirst. They are hot-tempered, and quick-tempered, and apt to give way to their anger; bad temper often gets the better of them, for owing to their love of honor they cannot bear being slighted, and are indignant if they imagine themselves unfairly treated. While they love honor, they love victory still more; for youth is eager for superiority over others, and victory is one form of this. They love both more than they love money, which indeed they love very little, not having yet learnt what it means to be without it—this is the point of Pittacus' remark about Amphiaraus. They look at the good side rather than the bad, not having yet witnessed many instances of wickedness. They trust others readily, because they have not yet often been cheated. They are sanguine; nature warms their blood as though with excess of wine; and besides that, they have as yet met with few disappointments. Their lives are mainly spent not in memory but in expectation; for expectation refers to the future, memory to the past, and youth has a long future before it and a short past behind it: on the first day of one's life one has nothing at all to remember, and can only look forward. They are easily cheated, owing to the sanguine disposition just mentioned. Their hot tempers and hopeful dispositions make them more courageous than older men are: the hot temper prevents fear, and the hopeful disposition creates confidence; we cannot feel fear so long as we are feeling angry, and any expectation of good makes us confident. They are shy, accepting the rules of society in which they have been trained, and not yet believing in any other standard of honor. They have exalted notions, because they have not yet been humbled by life or learnt its necessary limitations; moreover, their hopeful disposition makes them think themselves equal to great things—and that means having exalted notions. They would always rather do noble deeds than useful ones: their lives are regulated more by moral feeling than by reasoning; and whereas reasoning leads us to choose what is useful, moral goodness leads us to choose what is noble. They are fonder of their friends, intimates, and companions than older men are, because they like spending their days in the company of others, and have not yet come to value either their friends or anything else by their usefulness to themselves. All their mistakes are in the direction of doing things excessively and vehemently. They disobey Chilon's precept by over-doing everything; they love too much and hate too much, and the same thing with everything else. They think they know everything, and are always quite sure about it; this, in fact, is why they overdo everything. If they do wrong to others, it is because they mean to insult them, not to do them actual harm. They are ready to pity others, because they think every one an honest man, or anyhow better than he is: they judge their neighbor by their own harmless na-tures, and so cannot think he deserves to be treated in that way. They are fond of fun and therefore witty, wit being well-bred insolence" (*Rhetoric* II, 12).

Aristotle displays the same penetration and the same mercilessly true-to-life realism when he goes on to charac-terize old age: "The character of Elderly Men—men who are past their prime—may be said to be formed for the most part of elements that are the contrary of all these. They have lived many years; they have often been taken in, and often made mistakes; and life on the whole is a bad business. The result is that they are sure about nothing and *under-do* everything. They 'think', but they never 'know'; and because of their hesitation they always add a 'possibly' or a 'perhaps', putting everything this way and nothing positively. They are cynical; that is they tend to put the worse construction on everything. Further, their experi-ence makes them distrustful and therefore suspicious of evil. Consequently they neither love warmly nor hate bit-terly, but following the hint of Bias they love as though they will some day hate and hate as though they will some day love. They are small-minded, because they have been humbled by life: their desires are set upon nothing more exalted or unusual than what will help them to keep alive. They are not generous, because money is one of the things they must have, and at the same time their experience has taught them how hard it is to get and how easy to lose. They are cowardly, and are always anticipating danger; unlike that of the young, who are warm-blooded, their temperament is chilly; old age has paved the way for cowardice; fear is, in fact, a form of chill. They love life; and all the more when their last day has come, because the object of all desire is something we have not got, and also because we desire most strongly that which we need most urgently. They are too fond of themselves; this is one form that small-mindedness takes. Because of this, they guide their lives too much by considerations of what is useful and too little by what is noble — for the useful is what is good for oneself, and the noble what is good absolutely. They are not shy, but shameless rather; caring less for what is noble than for what is useful, they have contempt for what people may think of them. They lack confidence in the future; partly through experience — for most things go wrong, or anyhow turn out worse than one expects; and partly because of their cowardice. They live by memory rather than by hope; for what is left to them of life is but little as compared with the long past; and hope is of the future, memory of the past. This again, is the cause of their loquacity; they are continually talking of the past, because they enjoy remembering it. Their fits of anger are sudden but feeble. Their sensual passions have either altogether gone or have lost their vigor: consequently they do not feel their passions much, and their actions are inspired less by what they do feel than by the love of gain. Hence men at this time of life are often supposed to have a self-controlled character; the fact is that their passions have slackened, and they are slaves to the love of gain. They guide their lives by reasoning more than by moral feeling; reasoning being directed to utility and moral feeling to moral goodness. If they wrong others, they mean to injure them, not to insult them. Old men may feel pity, as well as young men, but not for the same reason. Young men feel it out of kindness; old men out of weakness, imagining that anything that befalls any one else might easily happen to them, which, as we saw, is a thought that excites pity. Hence they are querulous, and not disposed to jesting or laughter — the love of laughter being the very opposite of querulousness" (ibid., II, 13).

One cannot fail to appreciate the vital tendency of Aristotle's philosophy, which manifests itself in the fact that all life for him is permeated with meaning to its utmost depths, and this meaning is always pervaded with some vital potentialities. This outlook makes Aristotle a fearless and serene contemplator of life, however bad or terrible it may be. For to his way of thinking everything has its meaning, because everything that is material is in quest of its *eidos*, thanks to which alone it is comprehensible. And this *eidos* exists not only in people's heads, but specifically in life itself, in its ultimate depths. From this point of view even nonsense has its sense, just as a "shapeless" pile of sand cannot fail to have its shape, namely the shape of a pile. This does not at all mean that there is no nonsense. It certainly does exist, or can exist, but with the reservation that it also has its *eidos*, i.e., in this case an *eidos* of nonsense, without which one could not say of this nonsense that it was precisely nonsense.

Aristotle's fearlessness in the face of the nonsensicalness of life makes him serene; and his spirit is constantly submissive to the behests of life. But this submission by virtue of *eidetic* universality is at the same time the mastery of reality.

In antiquity whatever was considered beautiful, profoundly justified and natural was termed divine. Therefore the beautiful cosmos with its eternal beauty was necessarily thought of as something divine, i.e., as something maximally meaningful. There is no need to say that in this respect Aristotle was a true man of his time. If everything has meaning, it is divine as well, so that Aristotle's merciless realism was entirely congruous with his recognition of universal beauty, i.e., universal deification.

In his *De Natura Deorum* (II, 37), Cicero reproduces the following passage from Aristotle's treatise *On Philosophy*: "So Aristotle says brilliantly: 'If there were beings who had always lived beneath the earth, in comfortable, well-lit dwellings, decorated with statues and pictures and furnished with all the luxuries enjoyed by persons thought to be supremely happy, and who though they had never come forth above the ground had learnt by report and by hearsay of the existence of certain deities or divine powers; and then if at some time the jaws of the earth

184

were opened and they were able to escape from their hidden abode and to come forth into the regions which we inhabit; when they suddenly had sight of the earth and the seas and the sky, and came to know of the vast clouds and mighty winds, and beheld the sun, and realized not only its size and beauty but also its potency in causing the day by shedding light over all the sky and, after night had darkened the earth, they then saw the whole sky spangled and adorned with stars, and the changing phases of the moon's light, now waxing and now waning, and the risings and settings of all these heavenly bodies and their courses fixed and changeless throughout all eternity, — when they saw these things, surely they would think that the gods exist and that these mighty marvels are their handiwork'" (*Cicero in 28 Volumes*, 19: 215-17).

Such reasonings are only natural for a philosopher who deems eternal and pure Mind to be the prime mover of the universe. At the bottom of the scale for him is matter, which is not yet the being but the possibility of any being, and at the top is divine Mind, which although immobile itself moves absolutely everything down to the least trifle; moreover, separated though it be from matter, Mind pours itself forth into matter and creates its many gradations, while matter does not remain only at the bottom but is also the principle of the endlessly varied actualizations of divine Mind. The result is unquestionably a complete unity, or a kind of monism, where the topmost gradually passes into the lowest and the lowest gradually and in endlessly varied ways passes into the supreme. The apparent simplicity of this scheme gives rise to so-called "eternal questions".

As we have seen, Aristotle is a merciless realist, who keenly and fundamentally experiences life with all its imperfections, with all its ugliness and even monstrosity. No question arises where nature and life are full of beauty: supreme reason with all its Ideas is simply embodied to its full extent in matter and there is no ground for any dualism here. But such is only the cosmos, in which Mind at its utmost is materially realized and matter at its utmost is *eidetically* shaped. There arises the eternal and beautiful motion of the sky with its regularly rising and setting luminaries; it is beautiful, and the cosmos is the supreme work of art. But what is man to do with his earthly affairs?

The earth is in the center of the universe, and around it eternally and ideally revolves the indestructible sky. But the sky with all its heavenly spheres is above the one in which the moon, the luminary closest to the earth, revolves. It turns out that the entire sublunar region is full of disorder, of births and deaths, of joy and suffering, all kinds of perfection and all kinds of hideousness. How can one justify this perpetual chaos of sublunar being?

Aristotle does not like to speak of fate, insofar as pure Mind knows everything, future and past, and contains within itself eternity. Nothing exists for it besides itself, hence fate does not exist. As we saw earlier, fate for Aristotle is always only chance, only necessity outside meaning, an irrational and antirational force. However, although he does not adduce any arguments about fate in the mythological sense of the word, Aristotle constantly reasons about matter. But matter is precisely the extra-*eidetic* fact of the realization of *eidos* outside meaning. And everything that is outside meaning can never realize *eidos* in its full meaningful significance but only in a partial and hence imperfect, hence even distorted sense.

To answer the question of how one might justify the hideousness of life, one would need to grasp the full naturalness and the full primacy Aristotle ascribed to the *eidos* of each individual thing, and all the more so to all the ideas taken together, i.e., the supreme reason of the universe. For matter is only possibility. It can exist, and it can not exist. And if it does exist and, being the incarnation of an *eidos*, it embodies it misshapenly, the *eidos* is so powerful that it is nevertheless unaffected by any distortions in its incarnation. It would be more correct to say, according to Aristotle, that the *eidos* is not only unaffected by these deformities but on the contrary becomes richer, more saturated and energetic. The more intensely matter operates, the richer its *eidos* becomes.

Hence arises Aristotle's surprising inclination on the one hand to preach practical activity and on the other to find the highest human happiness in concentrated withdrawal into oneself, in intellectual self-contemplation. It would seem that the two are incompatible. But Aristotle's entire *Nicomachean Ethics* is devoted to classifying virtues as "theoretical", i.e., purely contemplative, and "practical". And although the practical virtues procure inner satisfaction, pleasure and happiness, nevertheless true happiness is wisdom wrapped up in itself and withdrawn from all practical activity. This view is not very comprehensible to people today. But for Aristotle such a state is the absolute foundation for experiencing and loving life and for vital activity.

It is worth recollecting here what we said earlier concerning the correlation of *eidos* and matter. On the one hand, they are quite different aspects of being. And on the other hand, they are completely identical. Not only are they identical, but out of their identity is born what Aristotle calls life. Hence it becomes clear why the imperfection of life is quite justified by the *eidos* of life: they are after all one and the same — materially realized *eidos* and *eidos* itself. But one more step is now necessary to conclude our description of the complete material and *eidetic* unity of life.

If *eidos*, as the supreme foundation of life which justifies all its imperfections, becomes all the richer for them, then any imperfection of life only confirms the plenitude and variety of life. Life is a tragedy. For in a tragedy all sorts of mistakes and evils are committed and all sorts of failures and downfalls are depicted, but all these tragic imperfections and the death of the heroes only confirm and reveal the lofty meaning of life. Tragic purgation consists in the heroes' death arousing in us a sense of a higher justice. The heroes die, but thanks to their death we feel the breath of the laws of life manifesting themselves in the fates of the heroes. Thus, the identicalness of *eidos* and matter is not just simply a rational inference on our part. It is the tragedy of life itself. And if we initially said that the identity of *eidos* and matter is life and then showed that life is a work of art, the next step, according to Aristotle, is to recognize that this universal and universally human work of art is a tragic one. It seems to us that this is the ultimate conclusion of Aristotle's philosophy viewed as a whole.

# NOTES

[1] N.G. Chernyshevsky, *Complete Works*, Moscow, 1949, 2: 10.

[2] As quoted by Plutarch in his "Table-Talk" (VIII, 10, 1), *Plutarch's Moralia in 16 Volumes*, 9: 203-05.

[3] These quotes, which form part of fragment 80, are from Seneca's "Moral Essays" (I, 9, 2 and III, 3, 1), *Seneca in 10 Volumes*, William Heinemann Ltd., London, 1970, 1: 129, 259.

## The Unanswered,
## but Most Important Question

At the end of our book one final question is left: what is the relation of Aristotle's philosophy to his life and fate?

In ancient Greece there does not seem to have been a philosopher with a more encyclopedic scope than Aristotle. He was a man who always looked first and foremost for the meaning of reality and formulated the truths he discovered as broadly and deeply as possible. In his zoological treatises he established and described over four hundred species of animals. In his socio-political writings he described 158 different Greek and non-Greek legal systems. The entire fifth book of his fundamental work *Metaphysics* is specially devoted to philosophical terminology, and each term appears with two or three and sometimes even five or six meanings.

His search for the meaning of life brought him at the tender age of eighteen to the richest, most developed and at the time most elevated philosophical school — Plato's Academy. At the Academy Aristotle mastered Plato's philosophy, but here, too, he did not in the least remain passive. He very soon developed a quite critical attitude to Platonism, whose achievements he was able to perceive as well as its shortcomings.

In Aristotle, the brilliant philosopher was united with a political activist. Aristotle was infinitely devoted to the interests of his native Greece, and with all his might wanted to preserve it the way it had been in its heyday. But he was to encounter a tragic fate.

The classical Greek *polis* was headed toward inevitable ruin. Aristotle was not a passive observer, and hoped the freedom of the independent city-states could be retained under the rule of the humane Macedonian kings. This dream had been frustrated because the Macedonian kings were in reality despots, desiring not a freely flourishing, democratic Greece, but its servile submission.

Having completely lost faith in the Macedonian rulers whom he had sympathized with and whose humanity he had believed in for a long time, Aristotle wanted to act. One cannot close one's eyes to the fact that the legend of Alexander the Great's poisoning by Aristotle may be true.

Perhaps Aristotle meditated poisoning him when he saw how soon he had turned from a philosophizing monarch and respectful pupil into a cruel conqueror and tyrant.

The problems which were tormenting Aristotle did not vanish with Alexander's death. What was to be done? He could still join the patriots fighting against Philip and Alexander and with them come to the defence of the ancient ideals. But here he met with a cruel disappointment as well. He had lost faith in the prospects which Macedonian dominion seemed to offer Greece, but reality destroyed all his remaining illusions. He lost faith in anything constant, noble and reasonable. For the enlightened philosopher the Greek patriots were useless conservatives, and for their part they saw Aristotle only as an alien and enemy and were ready to deal with him as fittingly as they had dealt with the too clever Socrates.

Aristotle was a strong person. And when it turned out that there was nowhere else to go, he presumably took poison and thus rid himself of insoluble problems.

Thus ended Aristotle's life. Yet all his probings and his entire life testify to the unprecedented staunchness of this great man, for whom even death itself was an act of wisdom and imperturbable serenity.

In studying Aristotle's biography in detail, one cannot fail to be amazed at how consistently and naturally his philosophy coincided with his life activities. As we know, his philosophy advances the theory of the four-principle structure of all being, or in other words, the ultimate identicalness of the *eidos* and matter of a thing. This coincidence of the two enriches not only matter, which without *eidos* would be merely empty possibility and not reality, but *eidos* as well, which without matter, i.e., without its actual realization, would also remain empty possibility.

Life is tragic. But the tragedy of life can be understood only by one who sees the *eidetic*, or ideal, reality in the depths of this tragedy. The fate of the heroes in a Greek tragedy attests to the existence of the supreme life principles, which alone are capable of giving meaning to this tragic fate. Aristotle proved as much both in his philosophical theories and in his practical life and public activity.

The reader has a right to wonder whether the relation of theory to practice found in Aristotle's life is the only or best possible one. There can be only one answer to this question. Aristotle's example is far from being the only possible one for us, and can hardly be considered the best. But how is one to live, where is one to seek the meaning of life, how is one to think? Reality is full of contradictions. What is one to do, when these contradictions seem perpetual?

All we can say in response is that the point of our book is to put this question boldly and sincerely. If the readers have taken it seriously, we have achieved our goal.

For us Aristotle represents an uncompromising and courageous answer to the question of the meaning of life. But it is clear that everyone has to seek his own way. Aristotle said that Plato was his friend, but the truth was dearer to him. Aristotle is our friend. As for what route to take in searching for the truth and surmounting life's contradictions, everyone must figure it out for himself. Each person must find the meaning of life by his own effort, through suffering.

# Name Index

193

# Subject Index